BIBLE-BASED ANSWERS TO

QUESTIONS
KIDS ASK

ABOUT

LOVE AND SEX

BIBLE-BASED ANSWERS TO

QUESTIONS
KIDS ASK
ABOUT

LOVE AND SEX

CHARLES MILLS

REVIEW AND HERALD® PUBLISHING ASSOCIATION
HAGERSTOWN, MD 21740

The author assumes full responsibility for the accuracy of all
facts and quotations as cited in this book.

Unless otherwise noted, all texts are from the *Holy Bible, New International
Version.* Copyright © 1973, 1978, 1984, International Bible Society. Used
by permission of Zondervan Bible Publishers.

This book was
Edited by Gerald Wheeler
Designed by Willie S. Duke
Typeset: Berkeley Book 12/13

PRINTED IN U.S.A.

01 00 99 98 97   5 4 3 2 1

R&H Cataloging Service
Mills, Charles Henning, 1950-
      Bible-based answers to questions kids ask
about love and sex.

      1. Sex education.   2. Love.   I. Title.

                  372.372

ISBN 0-8280-1255-5

Dedication

*To Dorinda,
the love of my life*

Contents

Contents

Foreword

OK, guys. You asked for it. Literally!

As I was writing *Secrets From the Treasure Chest,* the editors at the Review and Herald noticed the many queries sent in by young people across North America on a certain subject.

"Hey, Charles," they said, "what's with all this sex stuff?"

"Young people want to know about it," I explained. "And I promised them I'd answer every question. Seems romance and sex are hot topics. They want answers!"

"Then we'd better print a second book so all can be heard," the editors quickly responded.

It's my prayer that this edition will help you form a strong, spiritual foundation on which to build exciting, fulfilling relationships. This boy-girl thing is here to stay. Romance and sex offer great potential for happiness, and tons of frustration if we ignore simple, easy-to-follow guidelines.

So turn down the CD, slip off your cross-trainers, find a comfortable spot, and begin the journey. This is your book. You asked for it.

Chapter 1

Am I in Love?

Christian and Maryling stood side by side, looking down at the dark, swirling waters of a Miami canal. Night was heavy around them, but not as heavy as the feelings pressing against their hearts.

After a final embrace, they stepped out into space and dropped into the fast-moving currents. Neither knew how to swim.

Earlier that evening, Christian Davila, 14, had penned a letter to his parents. "I can't go on living," he wrote. "I'm escaping from the realm of reality into the darkness of the unknown. Because reality is that I can't be with Maryling."

Maryling Flores, 13, had jotted down her thoughts as well. "Mom and Dad, you'll never be able to understand the love between me and Christian. You don't let me see him in this world, so we're going to another place. Please don't cry for me; this is what I want. I want to feel happy, because I'm going to a place where I can be with Christian."

That afternoon the girl's parents had forbidden her to date Christian anymore, thinking they were far too young to be so serious about each other. Maryling hid an even deeper concern in her heart. She thought she was pregnant. But she wasn't.

On Saturday night, November 4, 1995, these two young people, seeing no other way out of their dilemma, ended their own lives in a watery canal, leaving behind heartbroken parents, tearful friends, and stunned teachers.

But wait. Weren't they in love? Isn't love worth dying for?

God, the one who created this very powerful emotion, inspired the apostle Paul to write these words: "If I speak in the tongues of men and of angels, but have not love, I am only a resounding gong or a clanging cymbal" (1 Cor. 13:1).

Then follows a description of this heaven-ordained phenomenon that every teenager and every adult should know backward and forward. If Christian and his friend Maryling had fully understood the very next words Paul wrote, they'd be alive today. Listen carefully. "Love is patient, love is kind" (verse 4).

It wasn't love that pushed those two teenagers into the canal that night, for love waits, it regroups, it finds a way no matter how long it takes or what obstacles must be overcome.

It wasn't love that created the headlines, got the coroner out of bed, and took away the joy of so many people. Love is kind. It never hurts others.

So what did Christian and Maryling have? What drove them to end their lives that horrible night?

The answer is complicated and often ellusive. But it does exist, partially in God's Word, partially in the human heart. If you'll stay with me, we'll dig together to find the hidden treasures of truth we all need to know.

What Did God Have in Mind, Anyway?

It began in Eden, that beautiful garden God created for earth's first lovers, Adam and Eve. After Adam's emotions had settled down a bit from seeing his newly formed bride for the first time, God invited the happy couple to "be fruitful and increase in number; fill the earth and subdue it" (Gen. 1:28).

What? That's sex! The only way to "be fruitful and increase in number" is to make babies. Was God telling Adam and Eve to have sex? Yes.

It seems we've uncovered a rather significant truth already. In Eden love and sex were interconnected. One didn't exist without the other. This was God's plan for the human race. Many of the qualities Paul penned in 1 Corinthians 13 concerning love would then also apply to sex. Both should be patient, kind, not envious, boastful, proud, rude, or self-seeking. Sex and love as God designed them would never delight in evil. They'd always protect and trust (verses 4-7).

But something happened between Eden and today. Something came along and totally messed up the Creator's perfect plan.

"It was Satan!" I hear you shout. "*He* caused the problems. *He* made two Miami teenagers who thought they were in love jump into a canal."

Not quite. Satan didn't push those young people into the water. Christian and Maryling, along with millions of teenagers around the world, are victims of a war that began a long time ago, in a garden, where two lovers decided that God's ideals weren't worth following.

Yes, Satan brought the temptations. He created the atmosphere of confusion. But the hand that plucked the apple and the feet that leaped into the canal were responding to deliberate choices made by minds who'd lost sight of God's ideal.

I want better for you, young people. I want you to have it all: love, sex, romance, a happy, long-lasting marriage, fulfilling relationships, pride in who you are. Yes, every bit of it! And you can, *if* that's what you choose for yourself.

Read this book carefully, prayerfully. Ask God to fill your minds with proper images of love and sex. Don't settle for anything less!

Chapter 2
The Sexual Me

BOY - GIRL STUFF

"I would like for you to talk about sexuality."
—*Darren, 15, Ontario*

Sexuality is what defines *male* and *female*. God set the standard. "But for Adam no suitable helper was found. So the Lord God caused the man to fall into a deep sleep; and while he was sleeping, he took one of the man's ribs and closed up the place with flesh. Then the Lord God made a woman from the rib he had taken out of the man, and he brought her to the man" (Gen. 2:21).

Next follow two astounding statements. Listen: "For this reason a man will leave his father and mother and be united to his wife, and they will become one flesh. The man and his wife were both naked, and they felt no shame" (verses 24, 25).

Sexuality: (1) was created to fill a need; (2) began in human flesh; (3) brings about a radical change in the life when combined with marriage; and (4) is nothing to be ashamed of.

Darren, you're a young man. From the top of your head to the tips of your toes, you're different from females. Why? Because that's the way God made you. But you're not complete. "The Lord God said, 'It is not good for the man to be alone. I will make a helper suitable for him'" (Gen. 2:18).

God designed men and women as a package deal. Through

marriage, human sexuality merges them into a condition called "one flesh." You're still male, and your wife is still female, but together you've created a new element I call "home." And only within this home can a couple fully express sexuality without shame.

1 + 1 = 1?

And what's supposed to happen in this union? "Have kids!" I hear you say. Yes, that's part of it. Child rearing is the ultimate achievement in God's home plan.

But human sexuality is not just about making love and making babies. It's about *uniqueness*. I enjoy being different from my wife. Through the years I've watched her strengths make up for my weaknesses, and I've seen my simple abilities complement her needs. That's what God had in mind when He said, "They will become one flesh" (Gen. 2:24). My wife and I can accomplish more together than we could apart.

We males and females can laugh at our differences, joke about how we react uniquely to certain situations, or even poke fun at the confusion we sometimes feel in dealing with each other. But we must never, *ever* consider someone better, smarter, more qualified, or in any way superior based on whether they wear a dress or boxer shorts. To do so is offensive to the God who made us unique by designing our sexuality.

"There is neither Jew nor Greek, slave nor free, male nor female, for you are all one in Christ Jesus" (Gal. 3:28). Different, but the same. Two people, but one flesh.

Macho Dude

Looking at sexuality only in terms of the *physical* differences between men and women is like standing with your nose pressed against a tree and saying, "What a lovely forest."

TV programs and movies shamelessly exploit women's bodies. Books and magazines show men as aggressors, the more violent the better. Advertisers target teens with suggestions that "if you wear these clothes, or buy this particular product, it'll make you more attractive to the opposite sex." So guys begin judging their worth by how many girls they "conquer," and girls think they don't have value unless boys hound them for dates. We make sex the yardstick with which we measure our importance.

Meaningful friendships, opportunities to practice gentle manners, and the chance to discover important life lessons get trampled by the rush to be totally cool, in, hot, with it . . . or whatever. We're staring at a tree and thinking we see the forest.

What I'm saying, Darren, is Don't get stuck in the narrow view of sexuality. Place God in the picture. Consider *all* the reasons He made guys different from girls. And then preserve and defend the purity of those differences, whatever they may be.

"The body is not meant for sexual immorality, but for the Lord, and the Lord for the body" (1 Cor. 6:13).

Isn't it nice to know that the God of the universe wants you to enjoy your sexuality—as long as you use it to fulfill His wonderful plan for your life?

"Why do girls have to go through weird stages? How come boys have it easier?" —Cleora Rose, 12, New Mexico

Growing up is a pain. Has been ever since sin entered the world. Your mind and body keep changing—sometimes overnight, it seems. Your likes and dislikes do flip-flops; even your relationships behave like mutant animals, evolving into either fire-breathing monsters or fuzzy little pussycats.

Then you look over at the guys, and they seem to be cruisin' along like everything's cool—that is, until they start to talk. Their voices crack, their skin breaks out, and they suddenly think they're supposed to be Mr. Macho with bulging muscles and facial hair.

Boys don't have it any easier in most categories. They just want you to think they've got stuff under control. In reality, they're as confused and frightened as you are.

Girls (and guys) have to go through weird stages because sin makes it hard to grow up. Satan wants you unsure of yourself, full of doubt, wondering what's right and what's wrong. So he relentlessly throws conflicting thoughts and beliefs at you. He makes you hate yourself and feel embarrassed about the changes happening in your mind and body.

But God is hard at work too, trying to get your attention with words of love, hope, and acceptance. "Now then, my [sons and daughters], listen to me; blessed are those who keep my ways. Listen to my instruction and be wise; do not ignore it" (Prov. 8:32, 33). Don't grow up confused. Grow up wise!

What's My Body Doing?

Perhaps your question has to do with the weird stages of *physical* growth that happen to girls and not so much to boys.

Changing from a girl to a woman can be an exercise in abject terror or curious fascination. Once you know why something is happening, the "weirdness" diminishes greatly.

The transformation has its roots in a command God gave Adam and Eve. He said, "Be fruitful and increase in number" (Gen. 1:28). In other words, make babies. In order to do that, a woman's body must develop in certain ways. Breasts enlarge to accommodate milk production. A monthly cycle of egg creation and release gets under way. Bones and muscles change shape, preparing to provide a nine-month home for future infants.

Stages happen in the girl's mind, too. God is preparing her for her role as wife and mother by strengthening her sensitivity to the needs of others, increasing her desire to be attractive to the same guy she used to beat up on the playground, and awakening in her thoughts of home and family.

At least that's the way it's *supposed* to be. This world, with its demands and distractions, can lead a woman in many directions. You have an abundance of choices for your life. But regardless of what path a woman decides to take, God's orderly sequence remains the same. "I will instruct you and teach you in the way you should go" (Ps. 32:8). God understands about the weird stages of growing up. He can help.

"Why do boys like to look at girlie magazines?"
—Kendra, 13, Alabama

Most preteen boys are simply curious about all the different shapes they sense hiding under women's clothes. When they see the naked bodies in these magazines, they find out, then wonder what all the excitement was about. But something changes as young boys begin to mature into young men.

God placed into the male mind a sexual fascination with and powerful attraction to the female body. In heaven's plan, this process was beautiful, wholesome, and natural. A guy would find himself smitten with a particular female; they'd fall in love, marry, and begin making babies. Case closed.

God meant sexual attraction to be shared between two people who had chosen to commit themselves to each other for life.

Then along comes Satan, who says, "If I can weaken man's mind through disease, bad habits, and disobedience to God's perfect laws, I'll be able to turn sexual attraction into a game, an addiction, even a sin." And that's exactly what he did.

Girlie magazines degrade women by flaunting their sexuality to anyone willing to spend a few bucks on such trash. The publications also degrade men by turning their thoughts away from the divine plan of love and marriage to mindless lust and selfish pleasure. "For everything in the world—the cravings of sinful man, the lust of his eyes and the boasting of what he has and does—comes not from the Father but from the world" (1 John 2:16). Boys like girlie magazines because sin is seductive.

Lust as God Intended

If you don't mind, Kendra, I'd like to talk to my young *male* readers for a minute.

OK, guys, listen up. Girlie magazines—you know, with all the pictures of naked or almost naked women in them—can be confusing. First I tell you sexual attraction is from God, then when you feel drawn to those magazines, you hear me saying it's a sin. What's going on?

God wants you to like sex. He gave you the urge to make love and designed you to enjoy kissing, hugging, petting, etc. But He also created a proper *place* for all this neat stuff to happen. That place is called "marriage."

When you gaze lustfully at a naked woman spreading herself across the staples of a girlie magazine, you're rejecting God's plan. You're abandoning His ideal for your life and leaving yourself wide open to Satan and his evil temptations.

You want to enjoy sexual thoughts? Then educate yourself, work at becoming a kind and loving person, commit to someone who loves you, then get married and have it all. Share sex in the safety and God-blessed sanctuary of your own home. Leave those magazines to the immature weaklings who aren't man enough to live life God's way.

"Flee the evil desires of youth, and pursue righteousness, faith, love and peace, along with those who call on the Lord out of a pure heart" (2 Tim. 2:22).

"What is PMS?" —Adrian, 12, Alabama

Premenstrual syndrome is a condition brought on by hormonal imbalances in some females during their menstrual cycle. Symptoms include depression, nervousness, anger, headaches, nausea, bad cramps, and tiredness. Even women will tell you they're not fun to be around while they're in that condition.

PMS is not a disease. You can't "catch" it from a friend. And not all women suffer from it.

If you think you might have this condition, see your doctor. A physician may have medicines that can reduce the effects of PMS on your mind and body, helping you to cope with this unfortunate problem. Also, if you know a teenage girl who seems to be mad at the world, angry, or simply unpleasant to be around, don't be too quick to label her as a bad person. She may be fighting her own burden of PMS and need gentle acceptance and understanding. Be patient. She probably has more good days than bad.

PMS, and many other problems plaguing our minds and bodies, serve as vivid demonstrations of the results of sin. God's universe exists in perfect harmony and balance. But when evil enters it, that balance gets lost, even within our bodies, and we suffer the results. But listen to this beautiful description of the new earth by our friend Ellen White: "The great controversy is ended. Sin and sinners are no more. The entire universe is clean. One pulse of harmony and gladness beats through the vast creation" (*The Great Controversy,* p. 678). God will restore the balance in all bodies, both heavenly and human.

Chapter 3

Hey, You're Cute!

"How do you know a guy likes you?"
— Erika, 14, Oklahoma

There comes a time when boys and girls become real mysteries to each other. It starts when they're around 11 or 12 and . . . well, never ends. I've been trying to figure out my wife for more than 14 years. Sometimes I don't think I'm making any headway at all.

Whether someone likes you or not is one of those mysteries teens continually face. But there are telltale signs to watch for. If a guy keeps bugging you for no important reason, pops up in the same places you frequent throughout your day, talks about you to his friends, glances your way often during class, or tries to embarrass you in a joking manner, then acts embarrassed if you confront him, bingo!

Liking someone is easy. *Showing* your regard for that person is kind of a challenge in the early teen years. Most guys (and girls) aren't exactly sure themselves what's going on inside their minds concerning the opposite sex. But even in this confusion, couples somehow find each other.

"I will get up now and go about the city, through its streets and squares; I will search for the one my heart loves" (S. of Sol. 3:2).

Be patient, Erika. If a guy truly likes you, he'll find a way to let you know. Just be open-minded enough to read the signs and realize that some males may be very serious while being really, really strange.

"How long should a Christian girl wait to start dating?"
—*Tasha, 11, California*

First, let's decide on a working definition of the word "dating." How's this? Dating is a boy and a girl choosing to enjoy an event, activity, place, or adventure together.

Such dating carries with it a lot of responsibilities. It may involve expenses, some travel, decisions to be made, feelings to protect, security concerns, and personal standards to consider. Who handles which of the above isn't important, but each item must be seriously taken into account, whether you're a Christian or not.

Listen to this great advice from the Bible: "Be devoted to one another in brotherly love. Honor one another above yourselves" (Rom. 12:10).

• A young person is old enough to date when he or she has demonstrated a willingness to put the happiness and comfort of another person first. Such a mature attitude guarantees the most fun in any social encounter. That's why alcohol has no place on a date. It lessens a person's caring, protective nature and makes him or her selfish. Selfishness destroys more potentially terrific dates than anything else.

Listen, Tasha, dating, done right, is tons of fun! You learn a lot about yourself and the person you're with. But your parents or guardians must see that you *and your date* take responsibilities seriously. Only then will they risk letting you out of their loving control. To do otherwise would be unwise.

Dating Rehearsal

But why wait? Why don't you start *practice* dating right now? No one even has to know about it. Here's what you do:

You and some lucky guy decide to give this dating thing a whirl. So you tell him to call you that night. Sure enough, at 8:00 sharp the phone rings. "Tasha," he says, "would you like to sit with me during lunch tomorrow?" And you say, "Who is this?" And he says, "Stop foolin' around, possum-brain; I'm asking you for a date!" And you say, "OK. Where shall I meet you?" And he says, "By the milk machines." And you say, "Chocolate or 2 percent?" And he says, "Give me a break, Tasha. This was your idea!" And you say, "Don't have a hernia. I'll be there. Thanks for asking."

The next day you're standing by the milk machines, and your friend comes up to you looking a bit nervous. "It's about time," you say. "My salad is wilting." And he says, "Sorry, had to wash my hands after cat lab." And you say, "I see you combed your hair, too. Looks nice." And he says, "I wear it like this every day." And you say, "Where shall we sit?" And he says, "Over there by the window."

So you and your friend have a date, and no one knows about it except your best friends, who are sitting across the room making kissing sounds into their fists.

Other potential practice dating situations could include family outings, school sporting events, church services, supervised nature walks at a nearby park, and even group shopping trips to the mall. Nobody ever said dating has to be just two people doing something all by themselves in some out-of-the-way location. Dating can be two adventurers enjoying each other's company in the middle of the New York City Marathon.

Remember, Tasha, you can create a date out of thin air even while faithfully abiding by family, school, or church rules.

Why not begin practice dating today?

"At what age should we have boyfriends?"

—Ruth, 11, California

Having a thoughtful, trustworthy boyfriend or girlfriend is the coolest, funnest, most exciting thing on earth, right up there with money in the bank and good health.

Like money in the bank and good health, creating and keeping a boyfriend or girlfriend takes work—lots of it.

To answer your question, I've known 11-year-olds who work harder at relationships than some men or women over 30. Age isn't the most important factor. Attitude is.

My grandmother didn't date during much of her teen years. She was already married. And she stayed married to my grandfather until she fell asleep in Jesus a few years ago. Seems there are people very capable of having boyfriends, girlfriends, even husbands and wives, at young ages.

But what about you? What about today?

The term *boyfriend* carries with it the idea of romance. Unlike dating, which might be two friends getting together to enjoy each other's company for a little while, being or having a boyfriend is more serious. Romantic involvement carries greater responsibilities and the potential for long-lasting hurt if you don't consider the other person's feelings and standards.

That's why you should always enter this whole boyfriend-girlfriend idea with care and prayer. The Bible says, "Delight yourself also in the Lord and he will give you the desires of your heart" (Ps. 37:4). Believe it or not, even *God* wants you to enjoy your boyfriend experience. And you can, *if* you decide right now to create your relationships around the ideals heaven has set for love in bloom.

What are those standards? Yup. They're found in our old friend 1 Corinthians 13. If you and your potential boyfriend use the guidelines presented in that beautiful chapter as your guide, your romance will be a fulfilling, enjoyable experience, no matter how old you are. I'm not saying you'll end up married or anything like that. But if your romance fades, it won't take your total happiness with it. Falling in love isn't difficult. God put in our hearts a strong longing to warm ourselves in the glow of another person's affections. But building a love that lasts and lasts requires all that the chapter teaches.

Ruth, you're probably going to fall for a lot of guys in the next few years. That's the way you discover the beauties of this God-given gift called love. Young men will sweep you off your feet, appearing like knights in shining armor, putting every movie star you've ever seen to shame. But take God's love standards along for the ride. Don't allow anyone to cheat you out of even one enjoyable, meaningful experience by asking you to loosen your hold on what you know to be right.

Look around you. Are the relationships you see working as they should? Or do you notice a lot of hurt in the lives of your friends and family? At the root of every broken heart you'll find the tattered remains of one or more of those beautiful ideals; I can almost guarantee it.

When you're determined to love God's way, you're ready for your first of many boyfriends. And Ruth, always ask yourself before you begin a relationship, *Is he ready for me?*

"If you like someone and he's just using you, what do you do?"—*Debbie, 10, California*

Oh, I hate when that happens! Makes you feel about as valuable as dandruff.

Trouble is, sometimes we *like* the person who's treating us so thoughtlessly, although, if you stop and think about it, that seems like a really dumb thing to do.

First of all, Debbie, you've got to truly believe that you are valuable, even if that person makes you wonder about it.

His view of you is extremely narrow. He's missing more than he's getting.

Second, people who use other people are trying to make up for their own shortcomings. They're basically selfish, so don't expect too much from your relationship.

Third, don't become like him yourself. It's easy to say "Well, he's using me, so I'll use him." Bad idea. Then you'll both end up acting like jerks.

Fourth, forgive. Your friend may have some serious emotional problems deep inside. He'll have to resolve them before he has a chance at happiness. Feel sorry for him, Debbie, but don't stay glued in that relationship for too long. Usually when good mixes with bad, bad wins.

And finally, ask God for guidance. He cares about your self-centered friend even more than you do. Ask your heavenly Father to attempt some surgery.

Surgery?

"I will give you a new heart and put a new spirit in you; I will remove from you your heart of stone and give you a heart of flesh" (Eze. 36:26).

If the operation is a success, your friend will need a kind, thoughtful nurse. Would you happen to know of anyone who'd like the job?

"I have two questions. First, is it OK to have a girlfriend older than you by three years?" —*Danny, 13, Florida*

Sure. Happens all the time. But the fact that you're asking this makes me wonder if perhaps your situation may be unusual.

What do your parents say, Danny? Sometimes parents view "older women" with a bit of nervousness. Perhaps you're not ready for the commitment the girl seeks. Usually, the older you get, the more serious you are about relationships. While you're having fun dating around, learning boy-girl communication skills and social graces, she might be wanting you to settle down, pay full-time attention to her, stuff like that.

While her requirements are perfectly acceptable, those around you may think you need more time to be the terrific 13-year-old guy you happen to be.

Now, don't get all flustered because someone doesn't see things the way you do. You're going to face that particular challenge all your life. Just relax and take it slow. Ask the girl to be patient. If she says, "It's now or never," you've just discovered something important about her. She's not committed to you!

If all of the above doesn't apply to you, enjoy being with the new "old woman" in your life. In matters of the heart, age doesn't count. When I was in first grade, my wife was just being born! We're working out all right.

"Here's my second question. Is it OK to sleep in the same bed with your girlfriend but not have sex with her?"

Well, it's certainly *possible,* if that's what you mean. But whether it's a good idea or not is a whole other matter.

Danny, God created boy people to sleep with girl people. Sex was His idea, remember? He gave us each special body parts and everything! So when we crawl under the covers with a member of the opposite sex, we're doing exactly what a loving God designed our bodies to do.

But the Creator also knew what a powerful, driving emotion sex was and how our bodies would react. So to make sure we men didn't go around trying to make love to every girl we stumbled upon, He created two important safety barriers for us to utilize: willpower and marriage.

You, and most teens, are supposed to be in the willpower

mode right now. Yeah, it's kind of tough sometimes, but remember, it's only temporary.

The other barrier is marriage. Here, you and the woman you've promised to love, honor, and cherish till death do you part surround yourselves with a protective wall of love and commitment that leaves you free to enjoy the sex drive to its fullest.

Sleeping with your girlfriend but not having sex with her sure seems as if you're attempting to wander around inside the wrong barrier. I can even hear God saying, "Uh, Danny? Aren't you in the wrong place at the wrong time?"

My advice? Unless you have the willpower of an Egyptian sphinx—which no flesh-and-blood boy has—stay behind the temporary barrier God created for you. That's where you belong . . . for now.

Chapter 4
The Big L
FALLING IN LOVE

"How do you know you're in love?" —*Erika, 14, Oklahoma*

First, we need to review several often-overlooked facts:

1. It's entirely possible to fall in love more than once.

2. It's entirely possible to love someone dearly and not have sex with him or her.

3. It's entirely possible to have sex with someone and not be in love.

Erika, I just want to make sure you understand that if some guy says "If you love me you'll have sex with me," you have the right to tell him he's full of hot air.

You see, people demonstrate love in many more ways than jumping into bed with someone. Salamanders have sex. So do roses, sorta. But you never see them picking out curtains together. The presence of sexual activity doesn't necessarily indicate the presence of love. Its absence doesn't prove anything either. You see, love is different things to different people.

However, there are certain guidelines for making love the most rewarding, exciting, satisfying experience on earth.

That's why God designed people to enjoy physical intimacy *after* marriage. He wanted sex to be an *expression* of love, not an *indicator* of it. God created sex to be shared between two people who have publicly promised God and human beings that their love is for forever.

A relationship built on sex has nothing to fall back on in times of trouble, and trouble always comes. It might be in the form of sickness, stress, disappointment, anger, even old age. Such elements can reach into a relationship and snatch away the ability or even the desire for sex. But two individuals who've promised God and other people that they're going to face the future together still have their love to lift them along. There remain promises to keep and dreams to fulfill.

In my work I sometimes visit retirement villages and nursing homes, preparing videos and brochures to bring in more residents. Often I interview the people living there, asking them what they like most about the community and the services they receive.

I've seen husbands caring for disabled wives and wives watching over bedridden husbands. For them, sex is now but a memory. But when you see them together, holding hands, smiling into each other's eyes, laughing, joking, sharing the day, you begin to realize just how powerful love is. Yes, they've had years to refine and strengthen their relationships, but the seeds of love, planted when they first met, have been growing, blooming, maturing in ways that hugs, kisses, and physical intimacies can't.

When two people allow love to build first, then bind their lives together in marriage, the sex that follows is simply icing on the cake. Sex doesn't sit up with you when you're sick. Love does. Sex doesn't bring comfort in times of great sorrow. Love does. And when Christ comes the second time, He won't be concerned about how well you performed in bed with your husband or wife. He'll be interested only in how well you loved.

With all this in mind, let's take another look at your question, Erika. You wanted to know how you can tell if you're in love. Here are some suggestions directly from God's Word. Every attribute appears in 1 Corinthians 13.

Love Is Patient

Are you willing to wait for love to grow without trying to rush it?

One of the hardest things for us human beings to do is wait. I don't like waiting at all! Get me in a long line at the bank or park me on the freeway during rush hour, and I'd rather be *anywhere* else. Why does God insist that love be patient?

Because it often takes time for truth to surface. I know a man and woman who married each other one week after they met. *One week!*

Now they're discovering all sorts of stuff about each other that they didn't know before, things that will keep their relationship from growing and getting better. For the rest of their lives they'll have to settle for a kind of *standoff* relationship, a marriage in which no more adjustments are going to be made to accommodate the other. That's sad, isn't it?

If they'd been patient, they would have discovered these problems long before they promised God and humanity that they'd spend the rest of their lives together.

So don't be in a big rush, Erika. Take your time. Let love simmer slowly.

Let me ask you a question. Would you rather fly in an airplane that someone patched together quickly overnight, or in a craft that was assembled carefully, thoughtfully, by a team of people looking for possible flaws along the way?

This patience must also continue to operate at full tilt *after* you have uttered the "I do's." People change. Successful relationships continually adjust to meet new challenges. Love built with patience has a firm foundation on which to stand and make modifications.

Slow down. Build your love over time. It'll make it stronger.

Love Is Kind

Ever heard a guy yell at his girlfriend? Or perhaps you've listened as a girl belittled her boyfriend right in front of everyone. That's not kindness. Those people aren't allowing love to get a foothold in their relationship.

To be kind means putting the needs of the other person first.

When a woman who'd been caught committing adultery was brought to Jesus, He allowed love to guide His words. While everyone else was yelling at her, cursing her actions, telling the world what a sinner she was, our Saviour took a very different approach.

He gently reminded her accusers that they were guilty of sins of their own. Embarrassed, the angry mob dispersed.

Looking around, Jesus asked, "Woman, where are they? Has no one condemned you?" (John 8:10).

The woman shook her head. "No one, sir," she said.

Quietly, gently Jesus responded, "Neither do I condemn you . . . go now and leave your life of sin" (verse 11).

Whose words do you think that woman remembered? The shouting mob's, or Christ's?

When a boyfriend makes a mistake, what motivates your response? If you allow kindness to choose your words and actions, you're feeling true love in your heart.

Love Doesn't Envy

I'm going to let you in on a little secret. I've never been jealous in my relationship with my wife. Is that because I have such a powerful love for her? Well, I do, but that's not the reason. It's because of the power of her love for me. She never does anything to make me feel insecure, unwanted, rejected. Even if I sometimes act like a jerk, she refuses to create an atmosphere of envy in our relationship.

Envy can be death to a budding romance. Let's say you like this guy. He is athletic, has muscles bulging out everywhere, looks like a prince from some Bavarian castle, and can melt your heart with a smile. (No, I don't have his telephone number.)

This fella takes a shine to you. Says you're cute, etc., etc., and you begin hanging out together. But there's a problem.

Every time you see another girl within 50 feet of him, you get all worried. You think, *Is he interested in her more than me? Will he run off with someone else while I'm not looking? Am I pretty enough, smart enough, rich enough, funny enough?*

Although you may not be aware of it, you're creating an atmosphere of envy in your relationship. You begin to try too hard to keep his attention. Or perhaps you make sly comments about other girls, putting them down, saying how they're all immature airheads. So instead of the sweet, kind, fun girl he fell for, you're turning into a cold, nasty person who makes more and more demands. See what I mean?

Envy destroys relationships. "For wrath killeth the foolish man, and envy slayeth the silly one" (Job 5:2, KJV).

Don't let that "silly one" be you.

Love Doesn't Boast

You see him on almost every sitcom one time or another. He wears open-chested shirts, tight jeans, and expensive jewelry. This poor guy can't open his mouth without something sexual sloshing out. He's cool. He's hip. He's boastful.

He's also a royal pain!

Boastful people turn my stomach. You can't trust what they say or depend on their actions. But that doesn't stop them from telling you how wonderful they are and what a pathetic moron you happen to be.

Puh-leeze!

Erika, as you fall in love, something wonderful happens to your attitude about the person on which you've focused your sights. You begin to protect him, and he begins to protect you.

How? First by word, then by deed.

Suddenly, the *character* of your friend takes on more value. You want to guard that part of him carefully. True love doesn't allow you to share boastful stories filled with sexual overtones with your friends after your last encounter with Mister Wonderful. He doesn't go around making up tales of conquests and victories concerning you, either. As love takes root, the purity and wholesomeness of your relationship grow in importance. This strange but beautiful phenomenon is God's way of letting you know you're on the right track!

From that moment on, even your actions serve to protect the character of the other person. Am I saying that sex isn't a consideration anymore? Hardly. Sexual attraction continues to get stronger and stronger. But it's kept in line, getting all primed and ready for when the promises are made, the marriage vows spoken, and a new home is started with God as a permanent partner. Remember, this whole love thing was His idea to begin with. He knows how to make relationships *and sex* work best.

Love does allow some boasting. My wife is beautiful, smart, attractive, a great cook, fun to be with, sympathetic, kind, considerate, and my absolute best friend. There. I feel better.

Love Isn't Proud

"Pride goes before destruction, a haughty spirit before a fall" (Prov. 16:18).

Pride has probably killed more relationships than anything else on earth. Why? Because the very first thing pride does is snuff out the flickering flame of love.

Love can exist only in a heart that puts the interest and well-being of another person first. Pride turns the spotlight onto self, creating a darkness beyond its narrow glow where other people easily feel left out, unimportant, rejected.

Years ago I sat in the fashionably furnished den of a well-to-do friend. His wife of a dozen years had left him that very afternoon to spend the weekend with another man. Their marriage was over.

"Do you see all this, Charles?" he asked with tears rolling down his cheeks. I looked around at the expensive end tables and lamps, big-screen television, deep-pile rugs, grand piano, crystal chandelier. Just outside, through broad sliding-glass doors, waited a bubbling Jacuzzi and sun-sparkled swimming pool. "It's all worthless to me," he said. "Without Mary's [not her real name] love, money and things have no value."

That's what pride does, Erika. It sucks the value out of everything else. A pride-filled heart can't love another person, because it's focused only on self and what it thinks it needs. All else simply doesn't matter. Pride kept my friends from forgiving each other, rebuilding their failing relationship, patching up their crumbling home life.

If you're interested in a guy simply because being with him would boost your popularity or make you more attractive in the eyes of others, beware. There's no way love can exist in such a situation.

But if you're willing to let go of your pride and like a person for the beautiful, kind, gentle individual he is, then love's got a fighting chance.

Love Isn't Rude

● Now, why on earth would God put this statement in His great love chapter? Of course love isn't rude. Everyone knows that!

Well, not quite everyone. Some guys have the weird idea that bossing a girl around, being macho and crude, behaving like a clueless caveman, is the proper way to show love.

Come, Erika. Let's say it together. "Hey, guys: *Grow up!*"

Jesus Christ, the greatest demonstration of love this world has ever seen, never spoke a rude word, never embarrassed anyone, never grossed anybody out, and never aimed His frustration at a person directly. When He did show His unhappiness, such as that day in the Temple when the money changers were making a mockery of the sacred worship services, He focused His attack on what they were *doing*, not on their characters. "My house shall be called the house of prayer," He shouted with tears in His voice. "But ye have made it a den of thieves" (Matt. 21:13, KJV). In essence, Jesus said in no uncertain terms, "What you're doing here is wrong. Stop, this instant!" He didn't say, "You lowdown, good-for-nothing idiots. You have no place in my Father's house!" That would be rude. That would be unloving.

We find a lesson here for all would-be lovers. Never attack a person. Instead, focus your attention on what the person did or is doing. "When you didn't show up for our date, I got worried that something bad had happened to you." Isn't that a whole lot better than "You're just a lazy bum who can't even keep an appointment"?

Which of these two statements would work better for you? "When you look at other girls, I get the idea that you're not interested in me anymore." Or "You're a thoughtless, mean person who doesn't care one bit for me. Why don't you pay more attention to our relationship?"

Rude words and actions have no place in a loving relationship, because they easily wound hearts. Express your feelings? Yes. But wrap your words with kindness.

Love Isn't Self-seeking

Self-seeking is another way of saying *selfish*.

We're going to be talking more about sex in a later chapter, but one comment a girl wrote fits here. She said that after she allowed her boyfriend to have sex with her, from that moment on, that's all he wanted to do when they were together—no romantic walks by the ocean, no fun dates at Pizza Hut, no visits to the mall with friends.

What a sad but accurate illustration of selfishness. This guy was thinking only of himself and the pleasure he took at his girlfriend's expense. It forced her to miss out on all the other fun things she enjoyed doing.

By its very nature, love is "other-oriented." Would you expect anything less of an emotion created by God? Everything that love does benefits others. The greatest joys lovers experience are those that are shared.

Sometimes in my work I have to travel without my wife by

my side. Believe me, I'm pretty pitiful. I work as fast as I can to get the job done so I can hurry home.

Once, before I even met my wife, I was shooting a documentary on a beautiful Caribbean island. The moon was full and yellow, playing hide and seek behind white, fluffy, silver-lined clouds. Palm trees swayed to the rhythm of a small band playing on the beach, where the waves swished softly across the sands. It was absolutely magnificent—and I was absolutely miserable. I had no one to share it with.

Love makes everything more exciting, more satisfying, more enjoyable for *both* participants, not just for one.

While I was walking along that beach, the verse we looked at earlier popped into my mind: "It's not good for man to be alone." I shook my head and thought, *You got that right!*

Love Isn't Easily Angered

Do you have a temper, Erika? I do, unfortunately. Every so often it rears its ugly head, and I have to pounce on it with all four feet.

Most daily newspapers brim with reports of men (and sometimes women) who forgot to pounce.

A house my wife and I once occupied sat very close to our neighbor's abode. Almost every night we could clearly hear the king of the castle yelling, shouting, screaming at his wife. He called her all sorts of names, told her what a horrible person she was, and warned her to straighten up and fly right or he'd get really angry. Yeah, like he was under control now.

We felt so sorry for that poor woman. She worked hard at the office supply store we frequented, always kept herself pretty for her husband, and never raised her voice once.

Erika, which of these people demonstrated love? This couple presented a clear example of this important quality. When we allow anger to drive our responses, even to things we have every right to get angry over, we're letting go of love.

"A gentle answer turns away wrath," Solomon states, "but a

harsh word stirs up anger" (Prov. 15:1).

How two people respond to each other when things get a little rough is a pretty good indicator of the strength of their love.

Love Keeps No Record of Wrongs

Oh, boy. Here's a tough one.

You and your boyfriend are out enjoying a stroll down the mall. The two of you pass a clothes store and you say, "Hey, check out that cool sweater. I think it would look nice on me."

Your friend chuckles and says, "Are you crazy? It'd make you look like a beached whale, kinda like that green thing you wear."

Now, just how fast are you going to forget that? A year? Two? Never?

Love, as the Bible describes it, forgives and forgets *right now*. Why? Because hurt feelings only get worse as they're reviewed over time.

Perhaps your not-so-subtle boyfriend is right. Perhaps you *do* look like a beached whale in that green thing—as far as he's concerned, that is.

I've worked out a pretty good system in this matter with my wife. After I put on my clothes and think I look pretty great, I saunter past my wife nonchalantly. If she glances up and says, "Are you going to wear that?" I smile and quickly go change.

Love has a short memory when it comes to mistakes and errors in judgment. "I, even I, am he who blots out your transgressions, for my own sake, and remembers your sins no more" (Isa. 43:25).

A loving relationship remembers much, but forgets more.

Love Doesn't Delight in Evil

No one in their right mind believes for a second that rape springs from love. Neither do child molestation, sexual perversion, stalking, sodomy, or any other form of passion that takes its cue from the devil.

Love has no place in such activities. Never has. Never will.

But don't try to tell Hollywood that. They're under the impression that love is somehow wrapped up in every evil delight. Scriptwriters and producers need to spend more time with their Bibles and less time with their editing machines.

Relationships that include any form of deviant behavior are void of true love. A husband who demands sex instead of nurturing it, a wife who dresses in revealing clothes in public to grab attention, pornographic magazines piled under the bed, X-rated videos waiting in the VCR, all suggest the very real presence of evil in the home.

Yes, evil can be fun, but only for a moment. Such activities may seem OK in the beginning, but soon you begin to reap the rewards. Heartache, disease, frustration, guilt, and even death are the payback for those who delight in evil instead of concentrating on finding true, pure love.

Erika, as you experience coming relationships, watch for signs that you or your friends are beginning to find pleasure in what the Bible considers sin.

But hey, I don't have to worry about you, do I? You've asked how to know if you're in love. Your standards are high. Wanting to know what *true* love is, you're not going to settle for anything less. So check out the very next part of our verse in 1 Corinthians 13. It says:

Love Rejoices With the Truth

The more you get to know a guy or girl, the more secret faults begin to float to the surface in the relationship. In other words, the "true you" starts to show through.

Love doesn't run and hide every time something that doesn't exactly match your own personal requirements pops up. It rejoices at the opportunities presented.

My wife is very shy. I'm not. When we started dating, she found out that to be with me took some getting used to. She'd have to do some things that shy people hate to do—getting up front before a lot of people, aggressively going after business opportunities, meeting clients, sitting in meetings, calling strangers on the phone. Those were all part of who I was, and she slowly began to adjust. Why? Because she loved me.

My wife and I were asked to produce an important program at the 1995 General Conference session in Holland. During the second Sabbath afternoon presentation, which was being beamed by satellite to hundreds of thousands of homes around the world as well as being watched by 50,000 people seated in the big auditorium, I suddenly needed to talk with her. She was backstage getting people organized, while I was running things out front. I motioned for her to come to one edge of the big stage so I could give her some instructions. Right there, in front of countless people, my shy, timid wife walked out in full view of everyone to get her message, then hurried back to deliver it. Satellite coverage, a huge audience, people everywhere, yet there she was with her gentle smile, looking down at me, putting her shyness aside for the good of the cause.

She'd discovered the truth about me and made the necessary adjustment. Dorinda didn't run and hide or try to make me shy and timid. No, she changed for me. She challenged a lifelong timidity because she loved me.

As you learn about your special friend, Erika, don't be put off by your differences. Accept, adjust, and rejoice.

Love Always Protects

"Greater love has no one than this, that he lay down his life for his friends" (John 15:13).

History is filled with stories of people who've done great and noble deeds for others. I'd like to share a family anecdote, one that took place before I was born.

I have two brothers, Bill and Bob. Bill's the oldest.

When they were quite young, the doctor determined that Bobby needed to have his tonsils removed. He was terrified. But then Billy stepped in and said, "I'll go with you. I'll have mine taken out too so you won't be afraid."

Off they went to the hospital together, trembling hands interlocked. No encouragement from my mom or dad seemed to ease their youngest son's apprehension. But when the older boy spoke, Bobby seemed to relax. "You'll be OK," Billy kept saying. "I'll be right here with you." His bravery was remarkable and was the only thing that kept Bobby calm.

After the short surgery, the two brothers were wheeled back into the hospital room, groggy from the anesthesia. Bobby looked peaceful and quiet as he slept. Moving to Billy's bedside, my parents looked at his face. Suddenly they saw a tear slip from the corner of an eye and move silently down his cheek. The bravery had been an act. He'd been as terrified as his younger brother. But he'd been there when Bobby needed him most, silently suffering by his side. Billy had put himself at risk because of love.

What are you willing to sacrifice for love? Pride? Personal fears? The things you consider important? People in love have been making sacrifices for centuries.

Love Always Trusts

One of the strongest pillars supporting true love is trust. Can your boyfriend count on you, come what may? Can he trust you?

I once got a "Dear John" letter. Well, actually it said "Dear Charles," but you get the picture. It was during a college summer internship program. I was traveling around the country attending camps for blind children, making a documentary and writing press releases about the camps for local newspapers.

Back at school was a girl I really liked. She'd promised to wait for me, said I was important to her, and no, she wouldn't run off with someone else.

She ran off with someone else.

When I got the letter, I sat down under a beautiful cottonwood tree to read it. Man, what a shock! I moped around for three days.

I'd trusted her. She'd promised.

Then I met a terrific girl at the very next camp, and life quickly regained its value. Such are the ways of young love.

But I'll never forget the feeling of betrayal I felt. When someone breaks a trust, it makes you hurt deep inside.

True love, the type required for a successful courtship and marriage, is absolutely trustworthy. Although it may get shaken, pounded, cracked, or even chipped, it still stands firm. Like the wise man's house built on a rock, the love God designed for us to utilize rests securely above the storm of life, holding two people away from the ruin of separation and divorce. Trust is the glue that holds lives together.

You know you're in love when you become as trustworthy as a rock. It's also an accurate way to judge whether someone else's love for you is true. Believe me. I know.

Love Always Hopes

Whenever I want an illustration of what this part of the verse means, I just have to glance over at my wife and remember our first year together.

You know how sometimes trouble comes in batches? That happened to us.

Within one month of getting married, I lost a new job (the company failed), I went deeply into debt moving my furniture around the country, our car self-destructed, and I landed flat on my back in bed, sick, living in a borrowed trailer. Out of work, out of money, out of luck. But, and I thank God for this, not out of love.

My wife fixed up our little home with what we had, cooked delicious, health-building meals, read to me while I lay under the covers, and spoke endless words of encouragement and comfort. I had nothing to offer her anymore. Nothing. But she believed everything would turn out OK. And it did. After I got well, we worked hard and landed back on our feet running.

"And hope does not disappoint us, because God has poured

out his love into our hearts by the Holy Spirit" (Rom. 5:5).

My wife never lost hope. Why? Because she loved me. Still does!

Love Always Perseveres

Wouldn't it be nice if this were a perfect world in which perfect people fell in love and created perfect homes filled with perfect children? Even the dog would be perfect. The Bible wouldn't need to include 1 Corinthians 13. Nor would I need to write this book so you and I could understand what that chapter says. Everything would be, well, perfect.

In such a world love would not have to persevere. Before you reach for your dictionary, allow me to quote from mine. "*Persevere:* to persist in a state, enterprise, or undertaking in spite of counterinfluences, opposition, or disappointment" (*Merriam Webster's Collegiate Dictionary*, Tenth Edition).

In this world, true love simply can't exist without this feature. Period.

My wife and I have a little saying that we utter whenever we do something really, really stupid. I'll look at her or she'll look at me and say, "Do you *still* love me?"

That little phrase has a lot of meaning. In essence, we're asking, "In spite of this dumb mistake, in spite of my sinful human nature, in spite of the fact that I deserve to be flung off a cliff, do you love me enough to love me some more?"

The answer is always yes.

Love perseveres not because it always feels as though it wants to or because it sees a great reward looming nearby. It perseveres because God has empowered it with His spirit of forgiveness and hope.

When you see your relationships beginning to last longer and longer; when you find yourself searching for the good among the bad in a person; and when your heart gets battered but somehow comes away even stronger than it was before, you're learning to love. You're learning to persevere!

43

Love Never Fails

First let me say that love does not require that a person choose to put himself or herself in unnecessary danger as a matter of course. A battered wife should leave her husband and seek the safety of friends or organizations trained to deal with such a tragedy. Likewise, if a girl finds herself being abused by a boyfriend, she should get out of the relationship as fast as possible. Yes, love can survive even these conditions, but nowhere does it say you have to stand with your nose pressed against it while it's happening.

In order for the words "love never fails" to work in a relationship, several conditions must be met.

1. Both partners must be committed to the longevity of the relationship.

2. God and His standards must be included.

3. Forgiveness must be exercised regularly.

"Hey, Mr. Mills," I hear you saying, "I simply asked, 'How do you know you're in love?' I'm not trying to get married!"

Erika, there are not two types of love out there, one for young people, one for marrieds. True love is the same for old folks, newlyweds, high school students, and the thirtysomething generation.

Dating, getting to know a lot of guys, discovering your feelings, socializing, and casual boyfriend-girlfriend relationships are one thing. They involve people you "like" a lot. But you're asking about true, powerful, long-lasting, God-inspired *love,* and that deserves as complete an answer as I can create. So stick with me a little longer.

To move from *like* to *love* requires a commitment to longevity. You can't tell someone, "I'm going to love you for the next few hours [or until next weekend]; then we'll see what happens." Love isn't something you *try;* it's something you hang promises on, commit to, take seriously. That's why love lasts and lasts and lasts, even in the face of tough problems and powerful challenges.

44

True love can't exist without God, either. Why? Because He created it. Love attempted without regard to God and His rules is like trying to build a skyscraper without blueprints. It might look nice, but I sure wouldn't want to live in it. That's why the Bible can make such a rash statement as "Love never fails" *only* if God has a hand in building and maintaining that relationship.

Because we're sinful human beings who do dumb things, say stuff we don't mean, and lose our cool, we have to have forgiveness.

Take a close look at the "loves" you've seen fail. What happened to commitment? Where was God? Was there enough forgiveness? I believe you'll discover great gaps in the relationships you review, rips that allowed sin, selfishness, and pride to flood in, smothering the final spark of something that was supposed to last forever.

It's true. Love never fails. But people do. I don't want you to be one of them, Erika. I want you to live a life filled with the love God created just for you, and for me. It's worth standing up for, sacrificing for, forgiving for. Love can survive years of disappointments, nights of sadness, and days of toil. When two people are in love God's way, all the powers of Satan cannot bring them down.

How do you know you're in love? Compare your feelings and emotions to 1 Corinthians 13. Review it verse by verse, item by item. If everything matches, or at least is solidly heading in that direction, congratulations. You're in love!

Chapter 5

Birds and Bees

SEX

"I would really like the true story of the birds and the bees. I know how it works, but I just want to know the story."

—*Jeremiah, 13, Oklahoma*

Someone must've been telling you the *untrue* story and gotten you confused. Thanks for checking, Jeremiah.

Sex—another word for the birds and the bees—was created right along with Adam and Eve. Yes, God originated sex. Why? For the same reason God made anything—for humanity's enjoyment. He also told earth's first couple to be fruitful and multiply. So sex was to be both an expression of love and a way to make you and me and everyone else.

Sex was part of a very big package called "marriage." Yup, God made marriage. Performed the first wedding ceremony right there in Eden. While the guest list may have been limited, the meaning of the service wasn't. Physical intimacy between husband and wife was to provide a special pleasure for them to share. It was one of the ingredients of the marriage mix and a way to do something Godlike—create another human being.

After sin entered the world, men and women came up with the idea that sex should be enjoyed *outside* of marriage, so this guy began sleeping with that girl, and this husband began lusting after his neighbor's wife. It was like taking one of the ingredients out of a cake mix, eating it, and saying, "Wow! This is a great cake!"

"Drink water from your own cistern, running water from your own well," pleaded God through the words recorded in Proverbs 5:15. He was saying, "Keep the mix together. Only then can you have your cake and eat it too."

A Mindless Substitute for Love

God probably shook His head slowly from side to side when He looked down on this earth and saw men and women disobeying His most simple commandment.

"That's not why I invented it," I can hear Him saying with a great heaviness of heart. "Sex was meant to be shared in the security of a loving marriage relationship blessed by My presence. You're turning it into a meaningless game. Please stop. I want to strengthen your relationships. I want you to be happy forever and to help you create a bit of heaven on earth. But I can't as long as you disregard the holiness of marriage and treat sex so mindlessly."

Making love with someone you're not married to is like slapping God's face and saying "I don't care what You want. I don't care about Your big plan for my happiness. I'm going to do what I want to do. Leave me alone."

An Old Testament prophet has a message for those who act so selfishly. "Let the wicked forsake his way and the evil man his thoughts. Let him turn to the Lord, and he will have mercy on him, and to our God, for he will freely pardon" (Isa. 55:7).

Sex saved for marriage keeps its value in God's eyes. But sex before marriage makes us all losers.

Details, Details

Just in case someone isn't as informed as Jeremiah and doesn't know how sex works, listen closely.

When a guy is sexually attracted to a girl (or a girl thinks a guy is *really* cool), that's God's way of making sure we end up with each other and aren't off trying to marry an elephant or aardvark.

The sex act is a natural, God-created method for male sperm to enter the female's body. It usually brings pleasure, and in marriage, where it belongs, it strengthens the loving bond between husband and wife.

A friend of mind likes to compare this bonding with what he calls the "crazy glue syndrome." Have you ever seen that TV ad in which a guy's hat is glued to an iron beam and he hangs in mid-air like some kind of idiot? He's trying to demonstrate the strength of his particular brand of adhesive. "Just takes three drops," the announcer states.

God wanted sex to be sort of like crazy glue, binding two hearts together through intimacy and shared passion. He made it powerful, too, with a little going a long way.

Outside marriage the sex act creates guilt and frustration. Why? Because that's not where God designed for it to be enjoyed. Sex outside marriage bonds us to another when we are not ready for it. And breaking off any prematurely bonded relationships can be as painful as ripping apart glued-together fingers. Crazy Glue (sex) works best when it becomes a permanent connection between two objects (people). The goal of sex is to help hold a married couple for life.

The passionate love scenes filled with heavy breathing and lots of moaning and groaning dominating Hollywood movies nowadays shouldn't be considered a standard to shoot for. Some couples make love quietly and meaningfully without all that melodrama.

Many married people enjoy happy relationships without even having sex. Sickness, stress, or injury can reduce the desire or ability for physical intimacy. A hand-in-hand stroll in the park is all they need. "Enjoy life with your wife, whom you love," suggests one Bible writer in Ecclesiastes 9:9.

That verse, in a nutshell, is the true story of the birds and the bees.

"Where does most sex take place? Why do boys like to have sex? Why are boys more interested in it than girls?" —*Melissa, 14, New Mexico*

Most couples enjoy sex in bed because it's more comfortable and private. Paul suggests, "Marriage should be honored by all, and the marriage bed kept pure" (Heb. 13:4).

I take it from your questions that "boys" means guys your age or somewhat older. They probably like sex for the same reason men do. It's pleasurable and makes them feel manly.

That's what God had in mind when He created it. Along with making babies, sex helps to build the male ego, motivating him to care for his family, work hard to provide for his children, and to protect his wife from harm. Having sex sets in motion a myriad of emotions—all designed to benefit the home and family.

And that's also why sex outside marriage is so damaging. There's no home, no family, no future to work toward, no one to provide for and protect. Instead, people ignore these God-given motivations, often time and time again. Then, guess what happens when the guy finally marries? He wonders why he's losing interest in the wife he promised to love forever and the home he promised to sustain.

Ever tried to use the same glue or piece of masking tape over and over again? It loses its stickiness fast, doesn't it? Before long, it has no power to hold anything together. Men and women who've misused the God-made crazy glue called sex sometimes find themselves turning to substitutes in an effort to keep the romance alive in their marriage. But nothing can compete with the real thing. Just ask the guy hanging from his hat in the commercial.

Boys tend to be more interested in sex than girls because they believe sexual activity, or encouraging their bodies to respond to sexual stimuli, makes them more macho and proves they're valuable and worthy of attention. Most girls know better.

Feeling turned on by sex isn't a sin. However, thoughtlessly giving in to it without regard for the time and place for which God designed it, is.

"There's this boy I know and he touches me on the stomach and hair and arms and legs and I don't feel comfortable with it. It's not real disgusting, but I don't like it. I'm the kind of person who doesn't like to say no. What should I do?" —*Girl*

Here is a real problem that goes far beyond the teenage years. Sexual harassment in the workplace and social circles causes terrible anguish across our country and around the world. (We will discuss this topic further in a later chapter.)

However, I don't believe your friend is sexually harassing you. He's probably being curious and trying to see how far he can go before you stop him. But his actions, if not corrected now, could turn into a far more serious problem in a few short years.

It looks as though both of you need to learn a few things about surviving in a sinful society. Let's start with the boy.

Guys, please listen to me. Girls are really neat and all that, with a softness and attraction that can drive us crazy. Sometimes when I look at my wife, my heart skips a beat and I find myself staring at her just as I did when we were dating. That's not evil. Women have been causing skipped heartbeats for centuries.

Listen to this really mushy verse: "How beautiful you are, my darling! Oh, how beautiful! Your eyes behind your veil are doves. . . . You have stolen my heart with one glance" (S. of Sol.

4:1-9). If you think that's embarrassing, try reading the entire book. It's right there in your Bible. Yup, the Bible.

Solomon was totally taken with his young bride. Their very graphic words of love go on for eight chapters! Read it sometime. (I recommend you use a newer version, such as the New International Version or *The Living Bible*).

Why did God put the Song of Solomon (or Solomon's Song or Song of Songs as it's called in other versions) in your Bible? To remind us just how beautiful *and romantic* love should be.

So don't think that your attraction to the opposite sex is a sin. It's a gift from God. But like all gifts, it can be misused.

The Proper Touch

Touching someone in a nonsexual way is a harmless yet powerful method to communicate a wide range of feelings. A sad friend would welcome the gentle closeness of a comforting arm. A happy hug, proud pat on the back, and a shoulder to cry on are acceptable ways to show you care.

Traditionally, men tend to be lacking in the gentle art of touching while women seem to use it effectively to benefit many.

But touching can mean a lot more than "I'm sorry" or "Don't be sad" or "Hey, way to go!" It can be the opening kickoff to a wide range of sexual activities. And that's probably why our questioner is uncomfortable with the boy who tends to get too close. She's not sure of his motives. And maybe, neither is he.

So guys, be real certain of your motivations for touching a girl. If the contact springs from a caring, comforting, or encouraging heart, don't hesitate to show your emotions with a gentle, friendly touch.

But if you're just curious, or turned on, or trying to show how manly you are, here's some sound advice from our friend the apostle Paul: "It is good for a man not to touch a woman" (1 Cor. 7:1, KJV). (Notice that he means outside of marriage here. It's perfectly proper within marriage. In fact, something would be wrong if we didn't touch our husband or wife.)

There's something else guys need to learn. Girls are people. They have rights, just as you do. If they say no to you, that carries just as much weight as when you say no to someone trying to mess with your motorcycle or carefully broken-in baseball glove. Remember, a girl's body is a *whole* lot more valuable than anything you can ever own. And they should have to say no only once. If you're any kind of man at all, you'll cease what you're doing *immediately*. To do otherwise reveals your immaturity and self-centeredness. When a girl says no, *stop!*

Values, Sparrows, and Woodpeckers

OK, girls, it's your turn. Our questioner wrote, "I'm the kind of person who hates to say no." I've got a very strong suggestion for her: *learn how to!*

Here's how. Most people who hate to say no get that way because they don't want to hurt anyone's feelings. They don't want to disappoint, anger, frustrate, or cause any type of emotional distress to another human being. While this is a perfectly noble trait—one we should all nurture—it does have limits.

It begins with a realization of value. You're valuable. Everyone is. No matter what anyone says, no matter what's happened in your past, you're a one-of-a-kind creation of God. That's the same God, by the way, who has prepared an eternal home for you in heaven.

You may have been kicked around, put down, even abused, by unthinking, uncaring people, but you still have great value where it counts most—in the mind of God. Listen to these wonderful words: "Are not two sparrows sold for a penny? Yet not one of them will fall to the ground apart from the will of your Father. And even the very hairs of your head are all numbered. So don't be afraid; you are worth more than many sparrows" (Matt. 10:29-31).

The other day my wife called to me from the base of the stairs. "I think a bird hit the glass," she said with a worried tone. "Will you go see if it's OK?"

I hurried out into the winter day and found a little woodpecker lying on the icy ground below the dining room window. Picking it up, I held it close to my cheek, checking to see if its tiny heart was beating. Sure enough, I felt some movement.

I carried it to the side of the house, where I waited to see what would happen. Occasionally cats wander through our property, and I didn't want the bird, who was in no condition to defend itself, to be vulnerable.

After a few minutes its eyes opened, and it looked around. "It's OK," I said softly. "You're just stunned. I'll protect you until you can make it on your own."

Why was I doing all this? Because, to me, the bird had great value. He was a creation of God, and so was I. What would you think if, later, that little woodpecker allowed other animals to abuse it because it knew that, once upon a time, it had run into a window and knocked itself out? You'd say, "Hey, don't think like that. You're still a woodpecker. You're still a creation of God. So you ran into a window. Big deal!"

Yet many girls allow guys to abuse them without saying no because they don't think they're valuable enough to have any say in the matter. But they're wrong. They have a say, and have every right to express themselves with force if necessary. A girl must never, *never,* blame herself for the actions of another person.

What about the woodpecker? It finally started trying to struggle out of my hands, so I placed it on a low branch in a nearby tree, where it sat for a long time. Then, as if remembering an urgent appointment in some distant forest, it flew away, body, mind, and value still intact.

Girls, say no if the actions of another person are making you uncomfortable. You don't have to try to figure out why, or wonder if you're just being overly sensitive or something. That doesn't matter. Say *no*. It's your right. And you have this right because you're valuable in the eyes of God.

Someday a guy will touch you, and you won't mind it at all, because he'll be in love with you and you'll be in love with him.

With his touch, he'll be saying, "I think you're valuable too." Until then, don't accept any substitutes.

"What's sex like?" — Male, 13

Ask 10 people that question, and you'll probably get 10 different answers. It's a pretty individual type of activity.

Some concentrate on the *hows* of lovemaking. "It's fun, exciting, rejuvenating!" That type of stuff.

Others will mention the way it makes them *feel* deep inside; their emotional response to it. "Sex makes me feel more like a man [or woman]."

Still others will highlight how it *draws them closer* to their spouses. "When we make love, we know we truly belong to each other. Our relationship becomes more special, more important, closer."

Sex fills different needs in different people. That was our Creator's plan. He designed physical intimacy to serve whatever purpose was important to us at the time. A wife may wish to feel needed and loved by her husband, and a husband may have a desire to feel manly, or macho. Both requirements find fulfillment in the very same sex act.

So don't think of sex as a one-size-fits-all type of activity. That's why comparing lovemaking techniques or experiences with others often creates frustration. "It wasn't like that for me," a person might say, thinking they've missing something important in their own relationship. Well, of course it wasn't like that for you. You weren't there. Your emotional needs weren't involved or even considered.

Sometimes guys or girls get together and share stories of their great sexual escapades. Not only are they flaunting their sins in God's face; they're also setting others up for disappointment if their physical intimacies don't turn out exactly the same way.

Wouldn't you rather set your own standards? Wouldn't you rather allow sex to be what you need it to be, and not try to compare your experiences with those of others? I sure would.

So when you're with a group of friends or classmates, and the conversation turns to the subject of actually making love, leave. Just say "Excuse me" and leave. If someone asks why, tell 'em, "I'm not comfortable talking about this subject."

They might laugh and call you immature, but you'll know better. You've just done a very mature thing, something that anyone who truly loves their spouse will do.

What's sex like? When you fall in love and choose to take on the responsibility of a life partner, and that person loves you more than anything else in the world, and the two of you have made that all-important promise before God and witnesses to spend the rest of your lives together, you'll slip beneath the covers and reach for each other. What happens next is *exactly* what sex is like.

"Why do some say it's a sin to have sex?" —*Male, 13*

Is it a sin to go grocery shopping? Of course not. My wife heads down to the local Food Lion once a week. If she didn't, we'd both be a lot skinnier!

Is it a sin to go grocery shopping on the Sabbath? Listen to this Bible passage in which God gives His people instructions on how to live holy, obedient lives: "When the neighboring peoples bring merchandise or grain to sell on the Sabbath, we will not buy from them on the Sabbath or on any holy day" (Neh. 10:31).

Grocery shopping on the Sabbath is a sin because it disobeys one of God's commands.

Sex, like buying Cheerios, is a sin only if it's done in direct disobedience to the law of God. Any other time it's perfectly OK.

God designed us to enjoy sex within the safety and privacy

of marriage. He's got strong words to describe those who take part in it outside of such a commitment: adulterers, fornicators, lustful beings, self-seekers, sinners. Not exactly a rollcall for heaven, huh?

While God's endless grace and forgiveness can move someone off that terrible list in a hurry, why get on it in the first place? Sex, where it belongs, is not a sin. Never has been. Never will be. Like grocery shopping, it has its time and place. A smart Christian knows when to do both.

"If I have sex at a young age, should I tell someone? If so, who and how should I tell?" —Male, 13

God never intended for us to live our lives without help. When we get sick, we visit our doctor. Having car trouble? We head for the mechanic. Got a spiritual question? Our pastors gladly take our call.

Each of these individuals received training to help us find solutions. They've dedicated their lives to serving the public in a particular area.

Having sex at a young age (while unmarried) is certainly cause for concern. Why? Because something inside you has broken down. Your willpower, your relationship with God, your understanding of sin needs fixing. And not everyone is prepared to deal with such a situation. You've got to do some careful choosing.

Some very real dangers hide behind uncontrolled, free-wheeling sexual activity, dangers that can ruin your relationship with others, destroy your chances for future happiness, even take your life. So if you've given in to the temptation, you'd better establish some type of communication with someone right away.

First, consider your pastor. He or she might be just the person you need to see. They won't go ballistic, as some parents might. And their primary concern is the same as that of all moms and dads who love Jesus: for you to build a strong, healthy relationship with God and enjoy a happy life.

Perhaps there may be a teacher you trust, or a counselor at school who has proved to be your friend. Don't think you're going to shock them into not liking you anymore. They'll be thrilled to have a chance to keep you from getting into any deeper trouble.

Then there's good ol' Mom or Dad. You just might be surprised at their reaction to the news that their perfect son or daughter has slipped in such a way. Will they be disappointed? Sure. Angry? Perhaps. But they too will be glad that you confided in them. As I said before, the dangers inherent in uncontrolled sex are pretty serious. Your parents' reaction is certainly a whole lot better than AIDS or an unwanted pregnancy—a *whole* lot better! If you think you're man or woman enough to have sex, then you're man or woman enough to face the consequences of your actions as determined by your parents.

How should you tell someone? Truthfully. That's always the best way to reveal even the most painful secret. Ask God to stand by your side as you show the world how mature and strong you are by asking for the help you need.

More than likely, you'll find people who, as is God, are "gracious and compassionate; slow to anger and rich in love" (Ps. 145:8).

Should I get advice from someone before I have sex?"

— Male, 13

You'd think something as natural and God-blessed as sex would be easy. Unfortunately, for many that's not the case.

We have to remember that God originally intended for us to

enjoy marriage and sex in a perfect, sinless world. Love could thus exist without challenge or temptation. Men and women would entertain no thought of disobedience to God's laws.

Then we see a serpent in a tree and a couple eating forbidden fruit. Sin has arrived, and with it the degrading power of evil.

Today we live in a world filled with disease, guilt, anger, revenge, and selfishness. Believe it or not, such things can and do influence even the pure joys of what should come naturally to men and women.

Sometimes when a husband and wife try to make love to each other, many of these problems surface and affect their ability and even their desire, often to the point of making satisfying sex impossible. (Naturally, I am assuming that you are asking about advice on sex within marriage, as God intends for us.)

Under these circumstances a qualified *Christian* counselor could be helpful. He or she would try to help the couple work through their emotional problems and steer them to the One alone who can turn disappointment into joy.

Instruction Manual

Your question may suggest that you want to know *how* to have sex. *How do I do it? How am I supposed to act? What am I supposed to say? What's it supposed to be like? How do I know if I've done it right?*

Valid questions, they deserve valid answers. But you're asking the wrong person. You should direct such questions to your wife. And her investigation should be directed to you. Why? Because there is no universal method for having sex in God's world.

Nowhere in the entire Bible does our Creator give detailed instructions for making love. Nowhere. He didn't say to Adam and Eve, "Be fruitful and multiply, and here's how . . ." He left the mechanics to them, because He understood that the shared experience of discovering sex would create a beautiful, powerful bond between a husband and a wife. Finding out which methods worked best for them, they'd design their love life around their shared needs. Neat, huh?

"We have not received the spirit of the world but the Spirit who is from God, that we may understand what God has freely given us" (1 Cor. 2:12).

So, should you get advice from someone before you have sex? Yes. Ask your wife one question: "How can I best show my love for you with my body?" Nine times out of 10 that's the only advice you'll ever need to hear.

"Does God think sex is a sin?" —*Male, 13*

As I've said before, sex isn't a sin. Never has been. But millions of people use it wrongly. And that's what concerns God.

One day soon after Joseph's brothers sold him into slavery, he faced a rather serious predicament. His boss's wife came on to him like a runaway train. "Now Joseph was well-built and handsome, and after a while his master's wife took notice of Joseph and said, 'Come to bed with me!'" (Gen. 39:6, 7).

Our hero had an interesting response, one we all should use if we ever face a similar situation. Joseph said, "How then could I do such a wicked thing and sin against God?" (verse 9).

Sex wasn't the issue. Sinning against God was. The woman was married, and it's a sin to have sex with someone else's wife. Joseph was putting obedience to God before his own desires. After all, she was a beautiful woman. Potiphar was a wealthy man, and wealthy Egyptian government officials had their pick of the most beautiful women in the country.

It was a very real, very powerful temptation for Joseph. But he stood fast. He was just a slave, yet he knew that sex could be misused as a sin, and he wanted no part of it.

Our world could use a few more Josephs, wouldn't you say?

"What should I do if I see someone having sex and they're really close to me and I know they're not ready for it?" — *Male, 13*

There's something I learned a long time ago that you might want to consider as you try to help all your friends today and in the future. It's a simple concept, and I'm happy to share it. Listen closely.

You can't change people. The best you can do is give them information, inspiration, motivation, and support while praying that they—with the aid of the Holy Spirit—will change themselves.

Let's put this idea to work in your situation. First, information.

Our government has done a pretty good job of informing us about sexually transmitted diseases such as AIDS. Unless you live under a rock somewhere, you know the health risks involved in casual sex.

Also, much of this book is informational, outlining what the Bible has to say on the subject as well as offering *practical* solutions for certain problems.

Begin your "help" campaign by making sure your friends are discreetly informed about the moral and physical dangers surrounding their actions. Leave informational literature in places your friends frequent. Teachers and pastors usually know where to get booklets, flyers, or other material on the subject. If you find a TV show, audiotape, or video that highlights the risks, place them in your arsenal. Remember, you're only making the stuff available. You're not supposed to sit down and show it to them.

Next comes inspiration. I'm not talking about angel-singing, orchestra-playing, goose-bump excitement like you get at church. *You* can be the inspiration they need.

Confide in your friends that you're working hard to fight sexual temptations, and that come what may, you're staying true to your personal convictions. Keep in mind that it's not your job to pass judgment on their actions. A loving God will cover that part. Your task is to inspire with your decisions and unwavering determination. Of course, your heavenly Father can be your best supporter in this area, if you invite Him to be part of your team. "I will instruct you and teach you in the way you should go," God says. "I will counsel you and watch over you" (Ps. 32:8).

Motivation means providing positive encouragement. Have you ever had anyone motivate you? How'd they do it? ●

When I was a student at Middle East College in Beirut, Lebanon, a kind and thoughtful English teacher named Mrs. Hepker told me that I had the potential to be a good writer. I never forgot her words. To this day, whenever I see my name in print, I remember her powerful motivation. Mrs. Hepker, if you're reading this, thank you.

Your words can motivate your friends too. Perhaps they don't want to be stuck in a relationship in which sex robs them of other social and guilt-free pleasures. Maybe they're just waiting for someone to suggest exciting alternatives, such as group outings or helpful community service projects through school or church organizations. Offer alternatives. Then let them decide.

Last on the list is support. Where would we all be without the aid of friends and family?

"But," you say, "I can't support what my friends are doing!" And you shouldn't. What they're doing is wrong. Dead wrong. But they're still your friends and you mean something to them.

Many people, in their attempt to show disapproval of someone's actions or lifestyle, fail to support those areas that are harmless and perfectly OK.

I had a friend who asked me to teach him how to fly. So twice a week we'd head out to the local airport and practice takeoffs and landings, turns-about-a-point, stalls, cross-country planning, navigation, and all the neat stuff that goes with learning to pilot an airplane.

My friend was a gentle and honest Christian who loved Jesus with all his heart. But he kept his store open each week on the day the Bible said was God's holy Sabbath. He also was convinced that sinners, after they died, would burn forever in a fiery hell, something the God I find in the Bible would never allow. I even knew tons of texts to back up my beliefs.

Did all this keep me from being his friend, from teaching him how to be a safe and skillful pilot? No! We found a whole lot of common ground on which we both could walk and, in this case, fly over. If our conversation turned to religion, I'd share my beliefs and he'd share his, but we didn't press the issue. Instead, we'd tool along singing "Do, Lord" and "Amazing Grace" at the top of our lungs, blending our voices over the roar of the airplane engine.

You don't have to support everything about your friends. But in those areas in which you find common ground, you can be as true and strong a friend as humanly possible.

You say your companions are having sex and you know that's wrong? Then, maintain a safe distance from those activities. But in areas where Christ is an invited guest, support them to the hilt!

Remember, Jesus loves your friends even more than you do. Ask Him to be by your side as you try to inform, inspire, motivate, and support them. Good luck.

"Why is it so bad to have safe sex when you're not married and you really love the person?" —*Female, 13*

Recently I attended the wedding of someone who's very close to me. I've known him since he was just a little squirt riding his Big Wheel up and down the driveway.

The woman he married is a beautiful, thoughtful person who loves Jesus. Both have dedicated their lives to Christian service. And both were virgins when they said "I do."

There are many reasons for saving sex for marriage, some biblical, some medical, some social. But this particular friend and his new wife offered a powerful motive I hadn't even thought of. Let me share with you what they wrote to me when I asked them to reveal their feelings on this subject. Let's begin with the groom:

"For me, the primary reason not to have sex before marriage was not one so much of morality (although that played a major role), but one of demonstrated commitment. Because I saw my future wife demonstrate to me that she was able to withstand the sexual temptations of courtship and engagement (which were very strong at times), I now have more confidence that she'll be able to say no to someone else in the future if the temptation arises. Beyond that is the unshakable faith I have in her fidelity. I know that when she makes a commitment to carry through on something (such as marriage), I can trust her now and in the future, because she proved to me that she was worthy of my trust early in our relationship.

"That's security, and it comes in two ways. Either by the fidelity (chastity) before marriage, or by a long, drawn-out track record of proving one's self after the wedding (if you failed to wait). I'd rather do it the right way. I thank God that He gave us both the strength to wait. It wasn't easy, but it was worth it!"

I asked the bride to share her thoughts.

"I think the best reason for waiting is that now I can trust myself totally to my husband and feel no guilt or fear when I give myself to him. We can enjoy the relationship God gave us with guiltless abandon. I can't imagine the pain and self-consciousness that inevitably goes along with giving yourself to someone who may not be there tomorrow or next year. God knew what He was doing when He asked us to stay virgins until we were married."

What beautiful testimonies! Thanks, guys.

Why is it so bad to have safe sex, or any kind of sex, when you're not married and you really love that person? Reread what my two friends said. Think about it, then match their revelations to the dreams you have for *your* future. Next, prayerfully, honestly, answer the question for yourself.

"Why do parents make such a big deal about practicing safe sex before you get married?" —*Female, 13*

First of all, we need to get something right out in the open. There's no way on God's green earth to practice *safe* sex before you marry. The conditions just aren't right. Listen carefully to the following information.

1. "Condoms offer little protection against HIV infection," according to Dr. Saleem Farag, a Christian physician who works with the National Interdenominational AIDS Committee. He and many other health professionals work endlessly to inform young people about what he calls the "deadly lie" concerning this product. He reports: "There are 16 million HIV-infected persons worldwide who've been lulled into a false sense of security concerning HIV infection. Both the media and public apathy have fanned the flames of dangerous passions, resulting in immeasurable heartbreak and pain."

2. When you make love to someone, you're also making love to all the people he or she has had sex with in the past. That's the nature of sexually transmitted diseases. They spread from person to person without regard to who you are or what you think you know about your sex partner. In other words, you're risking your very life on someone else's actions. Seldom a smart idea.

3. Thousands of girls practicing "safe sex" get pregnant each year. So unless you're ready for diapers and 3:00 a.m.

feedings, wait. Becoming pregnant is an extremely real and all-too-common possibility.

4. Even if you happen to find a virgin who just crawled out of an autoclave, having sexual relations with him or her might be safe . . . but only temporarily. Without the commitment of marriage, what's to keep the person from having other relationships if the sex bug bites again? After all, you two are having sex. Since you're not married, you have no permanent claim on each other.

Now, with all this firmly in mind, why do *you* think parents make such a big deal about practicing safe sex before marriage?

Chapter 6

Sex

"When I was at another school, going out was the 'cool' thing to do. It was amazing the lengths people would go to get a girlfriend or boyfriend! Girls would take off their shirts to show guys their bras. They'd let their boyfriends put their hands in their crotch during lunch. Boys were always bragging that their penis was bigger than everyone else's. It was disgusting!"

—*Stephen, 14, Maryland*

Sex isn't supposed to be disgusting. God meant it to be beautiful. What happened to His wonderful creation?

The answer is surprisingly simple. The devil managed to turn sex from an expression of undying love . . . into a contest. The transformation began soon after Adam and Eve left Eden.

Cain, Adam's firstborn, had a son named Enoch. One of his descendants was named Lamech. "Lamech married two women, one named Adah and the other Zillah" (Gen. 4:19).

Seems the men back then wanted lots of children, especially sons. If one wife couldn't keep up with the demand, two would serve nicely. Or maybe three. How about four? Sex slowly became a way to populate the earth faster than your neighbor. At least these characters *married* the women first. But they were still operating outside God's plan.

Then along comes Solomon. Yup, that's right. Good ol' "your hair is like a flock of goats" Solomon. You ready for this? "He had seven hundred wives of royal birth and three hundred concubines [women available for the sole purpose of sex]" (1 Kings 11:3). In a rather blatant understatement, the Bible records: "So Solomon did evil in the eyes of the Lord; he did not follow the Lord completely" (verse 6). Oh, really?

Even today, in some countries, for a man to have one or more mistresses along with a faithful wife is commonplace, almost expected. Sex has become simply a plaything with which to demonstrate how macho you are.

Men and woman also use sex in more subtle contests. "I'll bet I can make you pay attention to me," they seem to be saying. "Not only that, but I can make you forget everyone else while you're with me." "I'm bigger, curvier, sexier than you!" everyone seems to be shouting at each other.

In this contest there are no winners, just frustrated and disappointed losers who wonder why they have a hard time creating a meaningful relationship with anyone after the games have ended.

Stephen, you're right. It *is* disgusting; not the sex that God designed, but the sex *games* so many people play.

The apostle Paul included this situation when he penned these motivational words: "Whatsoever things are true, whatsoever things are honest, whatsoever things are just, whatsoever things are pure, whatsoever things are lovely, whatsoever things are of good report; if there be any virtue, and if there be any praise, think on these things" (Phil. 4:8, KJV).

"What should you do if a boy tries to have sex with you

and you know you won't do it with him but you're scared?" —Female, 13

I went to college during the sixties and early seventies. Although that was before your time, a problem that existed then still affects lives today. That problem was drugs.

They were everywhere. LSD, marijuana, uppers, downers, acid—they had many names. They were touching most people my age in one way or another.

I had no interest in mind-altering drugs. My mind had enough to do to keep up with piles of studies and work at the college radio station.

Here's the interesting part. I was never, ever offered a drug of any kind. Though surrounded by young people who used them, they somehow knew I wasn't interested. I didn't even have to "just say no."

Perhaps there may be a lesson for you here. I'm certainly not saying that it's your fault that guys act stupid around you by trying to have sex. Those who pressure you for it have problems of their own that need addressing. But there are things you can do to make yourself less of a target for their selfish advances.

The female form attracts guys. They like all those curves and bumps. Tight-fitting clothes and revealing fashions don't exactly cool their fires.

Today girls find themselves walking a fine line between being attractive, which we all want to be, and being seductive, which sends out very powerful signals to male observers. You want boys to be drawn to you, but you don't want them to lose sight of the fact that you possess a mind and a soul.

I've seen young women heading for high school proms who literally looked like hookers. They shouldn't be surprised if their dates start to treat them as such before the evening passes. While the girls will tell you they were just trying to be pretty, their dates will nudge each other and wink knowingly.

"Hey," the girls will probably say, "I can't help it if guys have their minds in the gutter. That's their problem." These young women are right. But it's also going to be *their* problem too before the night is over.

A girl can be attractive without dressing seductively. Any guy will tell you that. But when a young woman dresses in a sexual fashion, the boy's response to her usually remains at a sexual level. She mustn't get all bent out of shape if her companion loses sight of the fact that she also has a brain.

The terrible truth is that we're sometimes forced to find ways around the weaknesses of others. No, it's not fair. But that's life in a sinful world. Choose your wardrobe carefully. Make yourself attractive, not seductive.

Say What?

Another effective weapon for warding off unwanted advances is how you talk. Do you use suggestive language filled with hidden sexual meanings? Are your words pure, free from curses and smut?

A foul-mouthed girl becomes a target very quickly. Why? Because dirty talk usually goes hand in hand with dirty deeds.

Jesus once said: "Out of the overflow of the heart the mouth speaks. The good [man or woman] brings good things out of the good stored up in [him or her], and the evil [man or woman] brings evil things out of the evil stored in [him or her]" (Matt. 12:34, 35).

In college, if I'd talked about drugs, thought about drugs, and gotten close to drugs, don't you think that those who promoted and marketed the stuff would have considered me a possible user of drugs?

If you talk about, think about, and let yourself get as close as possible to the sexual world, don't be surprised if that's picked up by weak-minded guys who'll try to take advantage of you.

On the other hand, if you fill your life and mind with

things of greater and more lasting value, such as educating yourself, learning a skill, or being of service to others, most guys will find you attractive for what you are, not for what hides behind your clothes.

No Fear

The last part of your question tugs at my heart the most. You said, "You know you won't do it with him but you're scared."

Listen to me very carefully. You are more valuable, more honorable, more deserving than any geek who tries to pressure you into having sex after you've said no. With that simple response you've given him two choices. Either he becomes a gentleman and backs down, or he becomes someone to be pitied. You mustn't be afraid of either one of these possible individuals.

Remember, you have to live with yourself after the date. You have to look in the mirror every day when you comb your hair. Who do you want to be? Who do you want smiling back at you in that reflection? Someone who's given in because of fear? Or someone who's chosen to control what happens in life, no matter what another person tries to do?

The expression "fear not" appears in the King James Version of the Bible nearly 100 times. It's there for a reason. Anyone who follows what he or she knows to be right, who stands firm in the face of temptation, who maintains control and doesn't turn the reins of life over to evil impulses or dangerous curiosity, has no reason to fear.

If a boy tries to have sex with you and you know you won't do it, push him away and say, "No, I will not do this, because it's wrong. I won't let you take control of my life, even for a moment." Then add, "You have a choice. Are you going to be a gentleman or not? Which do you choose?"

Don't forget to ask God to feed power into your words. After all, if you could see with angel eyes, you'd find Him standing beside you, whispering into your ear those life-changing words, "Fear not."

"I had sex one time with a boy. Now I have a new boyfriend, and he wants to have sex with me, but I don't want to. What should I do?" —*Female, 13*

You're in a very common predicament, not just about sex, but one involving many forms of sin.

We've all done things in the past we're not proud of. Then comes a time when we decide to clean up our acts and get back on track for heaven. Perhaps this is where you find yourself now. And to top it all off, your new boyfriend is probably saying, "Hey, you did it with that other guy. Why not me?" Right?

The great love chapter we've been studying in this book has a terrific suggestion for those of us who must face the mistakes of the past. Allow me to jot it down for you. Listen closely.

"When I was a child, I talked like a child, I thought like a child, I reasoned like a child. When I became a man, I put childish ways behind me" (1 Cor. 13:11).

Did you catch that? Paul makes a suggestion in this verse that should bring joy into any repentant heart. Children do certain things because they don't know any better. They make mistakes, get into terrible binds, sometimes even put their life in jeopardy because of ignorance.

Then comes the process of growing up. We begin to learn from our mistakes and discover ways to keep from making new errors. There even comes a time, according to Paul, that we "put childish ways behind" us.

Don't ever allow anyone to use what you've done in the past as a motivation for you to do it again. You've grown up. No longer a child, you're a new person with new values and new rules. That's the way it should be.

Even God, when speaking of those who grow in His love, says: "I will forgive their wickedness and will remember their sins no more" (Jer. 31:34).

It's never too late to change the way you are, to alter your values, adjust your outlook, spiritually move from childhood into adulthood.

So if a guy says "Let's do it!" and he knows you've "done it" before, you can lift your chin and say, "I learned from my mistakes. I don't do that anymore! If you want to be my boyfriend, you'll just have to live with that fact." If he says no, it looks as though *he's* got some growing to do.

"If you go to a party and a boy tries to have sex with you, what should you do?" —*Female, 13*

Here are some practical suggestions you might want to try.

First, choose your parties carefully. If it's unchaperoned or if no adult knows about it, you're putting yourself in jeopardy. You don't have to have moms or dads hanging around like zombies spoiling the fun. But they should be nearby and accessible. Their presence should deter a lot of guys from coming on too strong.

And if someone shows up with any type of alcoholic beverage or other drug, leave *now!*

Second, choose your date carefully. What kind of reputation does he have? What does he like to brag about, talk about, whisper about? Don't think he's going to change just for you.

Third, choose your wardrobe carefully. What kind of signals are you sending by what you wear? I'm not suggesting you cover yourself with a tent. Just remember to use judgment and lean toward the modest side of fashion. Yes, even teens heading for parties can "dress for success."

Fourth, choose your companions carefully. Peer pressure can literally kill. "Everyone's doing it!" your so-called friends might say. Well, you're not everyone. You're you, and you choose to control your own behavior.

Fifth, choose your limits carefully. Establish in your own mind how far you'll go with any guy, no matter how strongly you're attracted to him. If things start to heat up, change locations, change the subject, or change the atmosphere. As a last resort, change guys.

Most boys are gentlemen, although they may not want that fact spread around too much. Some need to be reminded of who they really are deep inside. And there are always one or two who have the manners and morals of gorillas. If the immature few begin to lose control, you take over *fast!*

And sixth, choose your exit carefully. Have a backup plan if all else fails. Know where you are and how to get to where you want to be. Keep in mind that there's one man who'll move heaven and earth to get you out of harm's way. He's the guy with one ear tuned to the phone just in case it rings. Yup. Dear ol' Dad.

If you don't have a father at home, find a worthy substitute. No one said we're supposed to live life on our own without some sort of outside assistance. Keep the telephone number of a trusted teacher, pastor, or other adult within reach. People over 25 can serve a purpose, even to a teenager.

Once you've done the above, you can enjoy your party to its fullest. Be noisy, jump around like an idiot, and have the time of your life. Youth is a blessed event that's only experienced once. So, party hearty! Just party smart.

Chapter 7

Why Wait?

Sometimes you get the idea that everyone in the world is jumping into bed with everyone else. Hollywood glorifies sex; books provide endless details; magazines advise how to enjoy it more; and chart-busting songs set it all to music. You begin to think that you're the last surviving virgin in a *just-do-it* society. Well, think again.

More than half the comments and questions I received for this book came from teenagers who've decided to stay in control of their sex lives. For those who say "Come on, let's do it—everyone does!" they have a one-word answer primed and ready. In a firm yet kind tone they simply say "No."

Why? For a lot of reasons. Allow me to share some of them with you. I hope you'll find encouragement and, perhaps, a reason to reverse the path you're presently taking. Listen to these young voices as they speak their convictions.

"I'm waiting until I'm married. There are so many diseases going around, like AIDS. Some kids will change

after having sex because they lose their childhood and they will feel used and old afterward."

— *Jennifer, 13, Maryland*

Interesting observation, Jennifer. Apparently you have friends on both sides of this issue and have learned a valuable lesson from their experiences.

We're *supposed* to change after having sex. God designed it to bring husbands and wives even closer emotionally. Outside marriage, though, that closeness causes confusion and frustration, to say nothing of a pretty heavy load of guilt. Before the vows a couple has no long-term relationship in place to support physical closeness.

"The Bible says [sex] is for people who are married."

— *Male, 13*

The Bible also includes stories of many who engaged in sexual activity outside marriage. In every instance their actions brought nothing but grief and personal pain. King David, a man who could speak from experience, offers sound advice to those contemplating turning from God's ways. Listen to his hard-won words: "Do not fret because of evil men or be envious of those who do wrong; for like the grass they will soon wither, like green plants they will soon die away. Trust in the Lord and do good; dwell in the land and enjoy safe pasture. Delight yourself in the Lord and he will give you the desires of your heart" (Ps. 37:1-4).

David knew how giving in to lust affects lives. He learned that when "the desires of your heart" were fulfilled God's way, the rewards were much more lasting and gratifying.

"I might get into a situation I can't get out of."

—*Jonathan, 12, Maryland*

What Jonathan is hinting at is unwanted pregnancy. Can you imagine what it would be like to be born to parents who didn't want you or felt you were a mistake? I know of one man whose parents blame him for all the bad that happens in their lives because they got pregnant with him and had to get married. "If it wasn't for you, we'd be living happier lives," they tell him almost daily. To hear such nonsense has got to hurt terribly!

By the way, notice I said "they" got pregnant. A woman doesn't get pregnant. A *couple* does. Anyone who thinks otherwise has a lot of growing up to do.

In his letter, Jonathan also stated, **"I've chosen not to be sexually active because I know I couldn't face my family again. Sex doesn't just affect you and the person you're sleeping with; it also affects people you don't think it will."**

Every case is different, but there are some striking similarities. They all revolve around one powerful emotion—guilt.

Please understand that sex is nothing to feel guilty about. But disobeying God is. Sex in marriage carries no burden of wrongdoing. It's as free and natural as the wind.

However, sex without the promises offered before God and humanity at the marriage ceremony is out of place and out of line with the Creator's plan for our happiness. It's a carburetor without an engine, a wing without a plane, a heart without a beat.

Guilt changes people. Surely you've experienced a taste of this type of transformation. Ever told a lie? How'd you feel afterward? How'd you treat people? How did it seem they were reacting to you? Think about it.

Under a load of guilt we do things we usually wouldn't do, say things for which we're later sorry. It changes us, and usually not for the better.

God's forgiveness can bump us back on track. But how much

better it is when we choose to stay on course from the start.

"I choose not to be sexually active because I'm not old enough to accept the responsibility of a possible child." — *Evan, 13, Maryland*

Evan, I'm proud of you. You've pointed out two extremely important aspects of this subject: sex brings responsibility, and that responsibility must be accepted.

I once visited an orphanage in Egypt. The kids were really great. They ran up to me and gave me lots of hugs, and we had a wonderful time touring their facility while I took pictures.

Then it came time for me to leave. I saw sadness on those usually smiling faces, a sadness that cut deep into my heart. In their world everyone who came left. Everyone they had fun with, played with, talked with, went away at the end of the day. These boys and girls had no mother or father to love them week after week, year after year.

Oh, yes, the staff at the orphanage did a terrific job of caring for their needs. The adults running the institution loved the kids as best they could. But there were so many children, and so few workers.

An unwanted or unloved child is like an orphan. When parents refuse to take seriously the responsibility of loving their offspring, sadness rules the day.

That's why God invented the whole concept of home. In a home in which love lives, there's safety and security for growing minds and bodies. If you take home away, it leaves children with a life filled with uncertainty.

Before you have sex with someone, ask yourself, "Am I, right now, willing to include a child in my dreams and hopes for the future?" Married men and women must ask themselves the very same question too.

And don't put a lot of faith in modern contraceptives (birth control devices). They only have to fail once, and fail they do—a lot!

"I know one girl who's only 14 and has been pregnant five times. I think that's a shame. She thinks it's cute. That's why I'm not sexually active." —*Female, 13*

I, like you, am trying to think of what's cute about being pregnant five times by age 14. Maybe it's the faces of five unwanted children being shuffled about from foster home to foster home. Or perhaps the young woman you speak of believes there's a certain cuteness in watching fetuses being cut up inside her uterus and dragged, piece by piece, out through her vagina and dumped into plastic trash bags at her favorite abortion clinic.

Puppies are cute. Unwanted pregnancies at 14 are not.

"I choose not to be sexually active because I just haven't found anyone worthy of my body." —*Female, 13*

I'd like for you to carry this comment one step further. How about "I haven't found anyone worthy of the body God created for me"?

We're not in this thing alone, you know. Each one of us has a heavenly Partner who cares more for us than we ever can. Our bodies and all the stuff they do are His creation. He maintains the miracle of life in our miles of nerves, pounds of skin and muscle, and vast network of arteries and veins. His power drives our heartbeat and sparks our thoughts.

"For you created my inmost being; you knit me together in my mother's womb. I praise you because I am fearfully and wonderfully made; your works are wonderful" (Ps. 139:13, 14).

When you give your body to someone, make sure that the God who "knit you together" approves of the match and can help you enjoy the experience to its fullest.

♥ ♥ ♥

And finally, here's a young woman who's really, absolutely, most assuredly, got it together:

"I choose not to be sexually active because I'm worth waiting for." —Kirsten, 14, Maryland

That's the kind of confidence God desires in us all!

Chapter 8

The Dark Side of Sex

EVIL LOVE

"I've been molested. I want to tell people, but it's hard. If it's so hard, should I tell at all?" —*Girl, 13, Montana*

When I read your question, I felt a familiar anger rising in my heart, a rage I feel anytime I hear of a child or young person being hurt or abused.

I'm so very sorry for what happened to you. If I could take away your pain, I would. I'd wipe the memories and embarrassment from your mind as well. But I can't. I can only offer you my tears and my prayers.

There is Someone, however, who's eager to do more for you than you may think is possible. You see, He's angry too.

David, the shepherd-boy-turned-king, once lifted his face toward heaven and shouted, "Who will rise up for me against the wicked? Who will take a stand for me against evildoers?" (Ps. 94:36).

After what you've been through, you may have felt the same way. "Is there no one to defend me?" you probably asked. "Doesn't anybody care about what happened?"

Often the most evil result of molestation is that the victim, not the abuser, feels the greatest shame. In embarrassment and confusion, the innocent people withdraw inside themselves, wrapping protective arms around their agonizing secret. Some live their entire lives this way, never allowing themselves to feel true joy, never letting anyone close to their torn and battered heart.

But wait! David has more to say. With a voice made strong from experience, he declares, "Does he who implanted the ear not hear? Does he who formed the eye not see? . . . The Lord has become my fortress, and my God the rock in whom I take refuge" (verses 9-22).

Listen, my young friend, you've *already* told someone about your pain. With your tears you announced, in no uncertain terms, every fear and frustration. The God who hears all and sees all has received your message loud and clear, and He's standing by, ready to help if you'll just give the word.

But He needs you to be involved in the process of healing. You've got to allow Him to utilize the talents of others here on earth—people who can be His supporting arms and His mouthpiece, speaking words of encouragement and love.

Begin by making sure Jesus has a place in your heart. He won't mind the anger you feel inside or the outrage simmering unseen. Gladly He'll listen to you scream out your frustrations or agonize over the undeserved guilt you may be carrying. Remember, He knows the true story of what happened. He saw it. And He understands that you didn't deserve to be treated so thoughtlessly.

Then ask Him to help you find a person with whom to share your feelings. It might be a trusted pastor, teacher, counselor, or health professional. That person doesn't necessarily have to have a bunch of titles following his or her name. In matters of molestation a compassionate heart and understanding spirit may be all that's needed to bring peace to your soul.

You also might want to check out the local groups who meet to deal with such problems. Many are church- or state-operated or -supervised. You'll be surprised at what a difference it can make to meet face-to-face with others who've experienced this terrible insult.

And if you have access to a computer with a modem, log

onto a couple on-line services. You'll find dozens of news groups and forums dedicated to this very subject. Once you are connected, the first thing you'll realize is that there are many people, young and old, who are dealing successfully with molestation in one form or another. Some write poems, some cry out their anger with heartrending letters. Others quietly offer consolation and encouragement.

After visiting such sites in cyberspace, I leave with a profound pride in the human spirit and its God-given ability to overcome terrible obstacles and then quickly turn around and offer assistance to others who are hurting.

Yes, you must tell people about your pain—the sooner the better. Ask Jesus to guide you to just the right person or organization. Then listen for Christ to speak the words you long to hear through them.

David wrote: "When I said, 'My foot is slipping,' your love, O Lord, supported me. When anxiety was great within me, your consolation brought joy to my soul" (Ps. 94:18, 19).

Please remember that in God, you have a friend who never fails. No matter what life throws at you, you are never alone.

Chapter 9
After the Fall

To close our book, I'd like to tell you a true story about a young woman who faced challenges I pray none of you will ever experience.

We'll call her Sarah. That's not her real name. The emotion in her voice over the phone as she recounts the past has the effect of fingernails on a blackboard—such pain, such scars, such incredible tragedy. Each word is a mirror into her past, and its reflection isn't always pleasant. Sometimes I find myself asking "Can God's forgiving touch even penetrate walls built thick by rebellion and reach into hearts where hope has been lost?" The answer is yes! When the Saviour makes contact, those time-built walls crumble and stony hearts melt. A new life begins. But that life must still live among the pieces of the past.

The woman paces back and forth, her hands twisting a handkerchief into contorted shapes. She glances around the back of the school auditorium and smiles at the small gathering of relatives. One calls out, "You look like you're meeting your first love."

Sarah stops and turns to the speaker. "I am," she whispers.

Outside a little red pickup truck maneuvers through the parking lot and comes to rest between two other cars. The driver sets the brake and studies the auditorium entrance. *What should I say? How should I act?*

He sees a small group of people emerge from the building. In their midst a woman stands looking in his direction. She seems nervous, almost fearful. *That's her,* he says to himself.

Sarah watches as a youthful form slides down from the seat of the truck. He looks so handsome, so strong and handsome. Tears sting the woman's eyes. *Will he want to love me after he knows, after I tell him everything?*

The woman shakes her head slowly from side to side. It wasn't supposed to be like this—life, that is. It didn't have to be. She'd been raised a Seventh-day Adventist Christian. Sarah remembers the tiny community she used to call home. It was just a farming township with friendly people and open smiles. When she'd been sent off to academy, the crowds there had almost overwhelmed her—so many people, so many choices to make.

Yes, choices. That's what it had been all about. She hadn't made the right ones. Sarah had turned life into one party after another. If she got lonely, she'd sneak out and walk the railroad tracks. There were always guys waiting there, ready for a good time.

Oh, she kept them on a tight leash. She was saving herself for marriage, for Mr. Right, for the one she'd spend her life with. But her actions didn't put her in good graces with the academy faculty, and soon she found herself back home attending the tiny public school nearby. Her graduation class was six students strong—three boys, three girls.

Sarah begins walking in the direction of the young man standing by the truck. She sees him start toward her. *What's he thinking? What if I say the wrong things? What if he hates me for what I did?*

The Adventist college she attended hadn't proved to be much

of a force for good in her life. Oh, they'd tried. There'd been Weeks of Prayer, small group discussions, Bible classes. But who wanted to read the Bible when there was much more fun to be had, much more adventure to be lived? Life wasn't for weak or dreary-eyed religious zealots. Life was to be experienced, right?

That's when she'd met Tom, an acquaintance from her academy days. His house was right near the campus. He invited her over one afternoon. She decided to accept his invitation—after all, it was her nineteenth birthday. His, too. They could have a party. That decision would haunt her for the rest of her life.

The boy watches the woman walk toward him. She's pretty, energetic. It is finally happening. They are meeting face-to-face.

Sarah draws in a deep breath as her thoughts keep drifting back over the years. That afternoon rendezvous at college plays again and again in her mind like an old warped and broken record. She remembers Tom's teasing, his taunting. The ridicule in his voice still makes her flinch.

Then she remembers the blood-stained sheets and crying out, "I'm not a virgin anymore." But Tom had gone—to watch television. He'd gotten what he wanted. Little did he or Sarah know that deep inside her a life was beginning. She remembers closing her eyes as if to shut the vision from her mind, but it has remained, enforced by the fact that that life is now walking toward her, across the asphalt separating the auditorium from the parking lot and the little red pickup truck.

The distance between them narrows.

The news had stunned her parents. She remembers the home for unwed mothers and the lack of love she felt there.

Then, during her eighth month, the doctor in charge of her case decided to induce labor. He was heading out on vacation and wanted to get the delivery out of the way before he left.

Sarah fought the anesthesia. She wanted at least to hear her baby cry before someone snatched it away into the arms of the people who had agreed to adopt it. Although she didn't know who they were, she was just glad her child would have a nice home.

But when the baby arrived, all she heard was an intern saying, "Looks like another one for the cemetery."

"No!" she'd screamed, surprising all in the room. "No!"

The doctor was able to stabilize the tiny life. And the mother heard it cry.

Now her baby boy had grown up into a young man. Sarah begins to run, her legs finding strength from somewhere inside. Joy floods her heart when she sees the boy do the same thing. The long separation is about to end. For the first time in 17 years she'll have the chance to touch her child, to hold him.

Suddenly they're in each other's arms, hugging, laughing, crying. "I love you. I love you," they say again and again. For one brief moment the guilt and anguish ease, their pain smothered by the mysterious web connecting mothers and their children, a web that time and circumstance cannot break.

Arm in arm they walk to the pickup truck and slip into the seat. The small gathering of well-wishers watches as the two drive away, out of the parking lot and along the road edging the fields and grasslands surrounding the campus.

Inside the vehicle a mother turns to her son and begins to say all the things she's longed to say—things held inside for so many years.

She tells him about his birth, about how she heard him cry. He encourages her, wanting to know all about this woman he's been told is his natural mother. As they drive along, the truth unfolds like a moldy, tattered old blanket.

The boy has a half brother, he learns. This time the father was a drunk, a wife-beater, a child abuser.

Sarah reveals how her life slipped further and further into sin—drugs, free love, sex clubs—how she worked for a time as a stripper, how one night a man held a knife to her throat and raped her for two hours. In the midst of the violence she'd remembered the God of her childhood, the God spoken of in the academy and preached about from the college pulpit. Even now she can recite the prayer she breathed. "Dear God, here's Your wayward sheep. I've hammered the nails into Your hands and feet again and again. If I'm to die tonight, please make it quick. But if I'm to live, I'll know You have a plan for me. I'm sorry for my life. Forgive me, God. I love You. Amen."

The son sits in silence, his young mind trying to grasp what he's hearing. His life has been so different—so very different.

"Two years after that horrible night," the woman continues as the boy listens, "I called my father and told him I wanted to come home. I could hear him crying on the other end of the line. My aunt had gotten the local pastor to visit me. He was so nice, so reassuring.

"The first thing I did when I got back to the farm was destroy all the trappings of my past life—the porno magazines, the music, my scrapbook filled with vile and shameful things."

As the little red pickup traverses the countryside, the boy begins asking questions. He wants to know if she thought of him often, if she ever tried to find him. Her answer is a quick "Yes, oh yes."

Then he tells of his life, of the wonderful people who are the only mother and father he knows, how they care for him. Sarah listens intently, basking in the realization that she'd made the right decision to allow her son to be adopted.

All too soon the ride is over. But two hearts have been blessed. Sarah would later reveal that her son's compassion and forgiveness made it possible for her to forgive herself. The young man would tell his parents that the deepest, darkest mystery in his life had been solved. He now had roots; now he knew who he was.

Today Sarah works as a nursing assistant in a Midwestern nursing home. At 43 years of age she expects the second half of her life to be a lot brighter.

"My first son was recently a student missionary," she'll tell you with a broad smile. "He taught people how to speak English. I'm very proud of him.

"My second son was raised by my sister and attended Adventist schools. He's studying to become a doctor.

"God answered my prayers by giving me my two sons in the best way possible—He's given them good homes with loving people to care for them. I just put them in God's hands. That's the very best place for anyone to be."

If you ask Sarah what her life has taught her, she'll quickly answer, "I've learned that God can return what you've thrown away. He can heal even the deepest wounds. God gave me the will to go on, to find hope, understanding, and forgiveness. He provided the strength I needed to forgive myself for what I did.

"I don't want others to hurt like I have. I wish I could tell every young woman in the world that if someone is mocking you or belittling you because of your standards or beliefs, they're not your friend. Get out of that situation fast!

"I still carry the pain and the scars. I always will. But now there's something else in my life. I know there's a God who forgives and loves. And I've asked Him to put me through whatever it takes to prepare me for heaven.

"I've destroyed my life. It's time now for Jesus to pick up the pieces and make me a new person in Him. When all is said and done, that's the very best choice anyone can ever make."

Young person, I want you to start making choices based on what you know to be right. If you've stumbled, God can forgive and rebuild. But if you choose to remain true to His perfect plan of love, He can give you strength to overcome temptation, peer pressure, even the taunts and jeers of others.

Determine today to make your connection with Him stronger, either by accepting God's forgiveness or by reconfirming your desire to obey Him, come what may.

Someday, wrapped in the arms of the one who has

promised to love you forever and has demonstrated that commitment by marrying you, you'll find a peace and a joy no secret relationship or backseat passion can ever touch. In the warmth and security of your new home, you'll discover what God had in mind when He created sex. With heaven's blessing, you'll find fulfillment. Under your Creator's protection, you'll find love.

Secrets From the Treasure Chest

Junior devotional by Charles Mills

Using God's Word, the writings of
Ellen White, and personal experience,
Charles Mills responds to questions like
those below asked by kids like you. Tough
questions about God, home life, school, relationships, church, and religion.

"Why is it so hard to talk to my friends about Jesus?
How can I get them to listen?"
"Why does God let some people live and others die?"
"Why does it seem that sometimes when you pray,
God doesn't hear you?"
"Should we love our stepparents the same as our own parents?"
"What should you do if a friend is doing drugs?"
"Do you think Jesus will come in our lifetime?"
"How do you decide what to do in life?"

Paper, 381 pages.
US$10.99, Cdn$15.99.

The Professor Appleby and Maggie B Series

Charles Mills and Ruth Redding Brand team up to bring you some of the best Bible stories you've ever heard—wrapped in a plot you're going to love!

An eccentric old professor receives mysterious boxes from his world-traveling sister, Maggie B. Boxes bursting with intriguing artifacts and life-changing stories of people who dared to stand for God.

Join Professor Appleby and his young friends to listen to Maggie B's stories bring the Bible to life!

1. Mysterious Stories From the Bible
Abraham and Sarah, Lot, Joseph, Rahab, Joshua, Hannah and Samuel, and Jesus as a child.

2. Amazing Stories From the Bible
Moses and the Exodus, Samson, Esther, and Jesus' miracles.

3. Love Stories From the Bible
Adam and Eve, Abraham and Sarah, Isaac and Rebekah, Jacob and Rachel, Ruth and Boaz, David and Abigail, and Jesus' first miracle.

4. Adventure Stories From the Bible
Samuel, Saul, David, Solomon, and Hezekiah.

5. Miracle Stories From the Bible
Moses, Elijah, Elisha, Joash, Josiah, and Jesus' miracles.

Each paperback features challenging activities and is US$8.99, Cdn$12.99. Look for more books in the series coming soon.

Available at all ABC Christian bookstores (**1-800-765-6955**) and other Christian bookstores. Prices and availability subject to change. Add GST in Canada.

The Shadow Creek Ranch Series
by Charles Mills

1. Escape to Shadow Creek Ranch
Joey races through New York City's streets with a deadly secret in his pocket. It's the start of an escape that introduces him to a loving God, a big new family, and life on a Montana ranch.

2. Mystery in the Attic
Something's hidden in the attic. Wendy insists it's a curse. Join her as she faces a seemingly life-threatening mystery that ultimately reveals a wonderful secret about God's power.

3. Secret of Squaw Rock
A group of young guests comes to the ranch, each with a past to escape and a future to discover. Share in the exciting events that bring changes to their troubled lives.

4. Treasure of the Merrilee
Wendy won't talk about what she found in the mountains, and Joey's nowhere to be found! Book 4 takes you into the hearts of two of your favorite characters as you see events change their lives forever.

5. Whispers in the Wind
Through the eyes of your friends at the ranch, experience the worst storm in Montana's history and a Power stronger than the fiercest winds, more lasting than the darkest night.

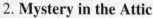

6. Heart of the Warrior

The deadly object arrives without warning. Suddenly Joey realizes he's about to face the greatest challenge of his young life. He's answered threats like this before. But never from an Indian.

7. River of Fear

A horse expedition brings Joey and Wendy face-to-face with the terrifying results of sin. Wendy goes for help, but soon finds herself in more trouble than anyone else.

8. Danger in the Depths

Wendy Hanson is missing. Her father and friends from Shadow Creek Ranch frantically begin to search. But every clue draws them closer to the unthinkable!

9. A Cry at Midnight

It's winter camp at Shadow Creek Ranch, and one camper's heart is frozen in pain. Exciting adventures help her discover a loving God who longs to heal.

10. Attack of the Angry Legend

It's more than 10 feet tall, weighs almost a ton, and is headed straight for the station! Your friends at Shadow Creek Ranch are about to meet one of nature's most ferocious creatures.

Paperbacks, US$5.99, Cdn$8.49 each.
